John Ellor Taylor

Underground

John Ellor Taylor

Underground

ISBN/EAN: 9783337186760

Printed in Europe, USA, Canada, Australia, Japan

Cover: Foto ©Lupo / pixelio.de

More available books at **www.hansebooks.com**

NATURAL HISTORY RAMBLES.

UNDERGROUND.

BY

J. E. TAYLOR, F.L.S., F.G.S.,

EDITOR OF "SCIENCE-GOSSIP," ETC.

PUBLISHED UNDER THE DIRECTION OF
THE COMMITTEE OF GENERAL LITERATURE AND EDUCATION,
APPOINTED BY THE SOCIETY FOR PROMOTING
CHRISTIAN KNOWLEDGE.

SOCIETY FOR PROMOTING CHRISTIAN KNOWLEDGE:
LONDON: 77, GREAT QUEEN ST., LINCOLN'S-INN FIELDS;
4, ROYAL EXCHANGE: 48, PICCADILLY;
AND ALL BOOKSELLERS.
NEW YORK: POTT, YOUNG, & CO.

1879.

WYMAN AND SONS, PRINTERS,
GREAT QUEEN STREET, LINCOLN'S INN FIELDS,
LONDON, W.C.

CONTENTS.

CHAPTER		PAGE
I.	INTRODUCTION	5
II.	TENANTS FOR LIFE	7
III.	INVERTEBRATE DWELLERS UNDERGROUND	43
IV.	UNDERGROUND SOCIETIES	67
V.	EARTH-WORMS	94

PART II.—OUR GEOLOGICAL RECORDS.

VI.	THE GENERAL STORY OF THE ROCKS	108
VII.	HEAT-FORMED ROCKS	117
VIII.	PROOFS OF UNDERGROUND MOVEMENTS AND CHANGES	129
IX.	ON THE CLASSIFICATION OF THE ROCKS UNDERGROUND	140
X.	THE PRIMEVAL LIFE OF THE GLOBE	147
XI.	NATURE'S COAL-CELLARS	166
XII.	THE MIDDLE-AGE OF OUR GLOBE	181
XIII.	THE WHITE CHALK OF ENGLAND	197
XIV.	THE LATER LIFE OF THE WORLD	210
XV.	THE "GREAT ICE AGE"	222
XVI.	FOSSILIFEROUS LOCALITIES	233
XVII.	CONCLUSION	253

UNDERGROUND.

CHAPTER I.

INTRODUCTION.

IF we had not been long familiarized with the fact, nothing would have seemed more strange than that the ground beneath us should have its peculiar set of inhabitants. We are accustomed to speak of the fish of the sea and the fowls of the air, but we rarely refer to the dwellers underground. And yet to many creatures the soil is their habitual home, just as the water is to fish, or the atmosphere to birds. If we removed them from it they would sicken or die.

Nor is this underground habitation confined to particular kinds of animals. Both vertebrate and invertebrate creatures make it their home; and although the latter are more abundant, they are not more wonderfully adapted to their subterranean existence than the former. The soil, like the atmosphere and the sea, receives into its bosom as tenants animals of various classes. The wonderful modification of the finger-bones, covered with skin, which enables a bat to fly, is not a more striking adaptation of means to ends than the peculiar structure of the bones of a mole's forelegs which enables that animal to burrow. Aërial and aquatic animals have their skeletons and members so constructed that we can tell at a glance the nature of the medium they are intended to live in. The same is true of the structures of worms, mole-crickets, and moles. So that we no longer need regard these underground dwellers as deserving of our pity. On the contrary, we ought to see in their special adaptation to subterranean existence, the operation of the same Wisdom which fits the bird for the air and the fish for the water.

This fitness of animals for a life underground may be found in all degrees. Some of them could not long live anywhere else, as the earthworm and the mole. Others seek a refuge, rather than a continual existence, underground, as the shrew, vole, rabbit, the fox, and the badger. Some creatures are assigned subterranean habits only for part of their lives, as the wireworms, and various other larvæ of insects. Numerous species of ants excavate their remarkable galleries, and conduct their well-arranged republics, underground. The humble-bee burrows in the hedge-banks, in order to lay there the foundation of its singular nest, at no small expenditure of skill and labour. Mason and other bees and wasps seek both underground shelter and convenience; and there can be little doubt that since these various creatures first appeared in the earth, in distant geological epochs, some have acquired many of the habits which it will now be our purpose to describe.

CHAPTER II.

TENANTS FOR LIFE.

AMONG the vertebrates, the Mole (*Talpa vulgaris*) may be taken as the type of underground animals. Whether we consider the structure of its fore-limbs, so admirably adapted for travelling beneath the soil, or the peculiarity of its silky fur, so arranged that it will lie smoothly whether we stroke it to or fro, and thus calculated not to harbour dirt or interfere by its friction with the Mole's subterranean movements, we cannot but feel that it is peculiarly constructed to live where we find it. Those who are apt to apologize for an animal "doomed," as they call it, to dwell amid perpetual darkness, might take a hint from Waterton's remarks on the sloth, which had been pitied by Buffon and other early naturalists for being fashioned in such an apparently clumsy and uncomfortable fashion. Nature needs no human apology—she asks only to be understood. But if men prefer to proffer pity where they should attentively study and observe, we cannot be surprised if their remarks appear frivolous to those who fully understand the subject. The insects which gambol in the sunshine, the minnows which sport in the village brooks, are not one whit happier than the Mole. Its very unlikeness to other animals is a proof of the highest wisdom.

Just regard it for a moment—its long, round body,

covered with fur capable of lying smooth any way, its pointed snout, short stout limbs, and small eyes nearly hidden in the head—for the Mole is not "blind," as many careless observers have imagined, although its eyes are rudimentary and small compared with those of its own order which live aboveground. But this apparent deprivation is benevolent. We have heard of men who have been imprisoned in complete darkness, and who complained of the acute pain caused by their aching eyeballs unconsciously straining after the absent light. The defective sight in the Mole, therefore, ought to be accepted as proof of its special underground adaptation. When caught, its bewildered habits in the sunlight perhaps cause it to appear stupid and awkward; but a fish is equally so when taken out of the water, and, indeed, so is any animal when we change its usual habitat. Now, examine first the peculiar structure of its forearms. The bones are short and strong, and the palms are directed outwards. The terminal joints of the toes are genuine diggers, and we have unconsciously imitated them in the steel instruments of gouge-shape which we use for rooting-up living ferns, and for garden purposes; that is to say, the terminal joints or claws are convex on the outside, and concave inside, and they taper to a point, as is usual in animals' claws. Each of the five digits is so fashioned that when they lie close together the entire hand becomes a strong shovel for excavatory purposes, actually contrived on the same principle as the individual toes. When at work the Mole thus excavates in front of itself, and is enabled easily to throw the soil behind it. Meantime its hind feet are not idle, and the observer may see that they are quite as remarkably adapted for burrowing underground as the fore-limbs. And as the Mole can use its body as a kind of fulcrum, it follows that the hind limbs can scoop away and cast behind the advancing miner all the material it hoes away in front. Notice also the *cylindrical* shape of the Mole's body—how well it agrees with other points in its anatomy, all of which plainly indicate a direct adaptation to a subterranean life. We know of no other vertebrate animal possessing so round a body. And it is evident that this shape, combined with the silky fur, must facilitate the progress of moles in excavation. Even the manner in which the hair is inserted in the skin of the Mole calls for special remark. In other animals the hairs are inserted at an angle to the surface, but in the Mole they are perpendicular. Hence the fur can lie backwards or forwards with the same silky ease, the friction of the animal's underground movements are reduced to a minimum, and no soil can lodge in its velvety coat whichever way it may turn in its burrows.

The great strength exerted by the Mole's fore-limbs requires equally powerful muscles to work them, and strong points of attachment in that part of the skeleton of the body with which they are connected. This is the case with birds, whose wings are their most muscular members. Their wings are worked by muscles fastened to the sternum or breast-bone, and the latter has a ridge or keel which is always developed in proportion to the bird's habits of flight, being high and strong in eagles, and scarcely visible in those birds which run instead of fly, and so use their legs instead of their wings, as is the case with the ostriches. Now, owing to the fact that the Mole resembles a flying bird in the great work performed by its fore-limbs, it follows that its breast-bone should be different from that of mammals in general (except bats), and we therefore find that it is thus fashioned on the plan of a bird, having a strong keel for the attachment of the muscles employed in excavating beneath the soil.'

THE MOLE (*Talpa vulgaris*).

Some naturalists are of opinion that the Mole uses its snout in digging. It is certain that this organ is always first brought into use, as if to detect which part of the ground is softest and best adapted for excavation. Its nose is extremely sensitive, both to touch and smell, and its peculiar conformation appears intended to render it of the greatest use to its owner. As soon as the Mole has smelled or felt out a likely spot for work, it commences to dig, and this so rapidly that its body seems to sink into the ground with a ghost-like disappearance. Whilst excavating its galleries the delicate sense of smell distributed over the inner surface of the long muzzle or nose soon perceives the presence of food. And there can be little doubt that the high development of this sense is compensatory for the low development of that of sight. As we have already remarked, keen sight would be worse than useless in the perpetually dark tunnels where the life of the Mole is passed. It has been frequently noticed that blind people seem in some degree to be compensated for their great affliction by the marvellous improvement in the delicacy of their sense of touch. Just so with the Mole. Its rudimentary and almost needless eyesight is more than atoned for by its powerful sense of smell, which appears to be to the animal nearly all the senses rolled into one. Its sense of touch also is notably great, for it can perceive the faintest tread or tremor of the ground in which it is burrowing, and can thus perhaps detect the presence of its food when the latter is moving about. Shakespeare, who in his boyhood must have often noticed the habits of the Mole in the meadows of the Avon, mentions its quick detection of a stranger, although he refers it to its sense of hearing:—

"Pray you, tread softly, that the blind mole may not
Hear a foot fall!"

And Mr. Bell tells us that mole-catchers prefer windy nights for setting their traps, so that the Moles may not hear their tread.

The chief food of the Mole is the common earthworm, and it is in pursuit of its prey that it leads an underground life. But whether it was the habitual preference for the earthworm as food which caused the Mole to adopt its peculiar mode of existence, and led it to invent its system of tunnelling and burrowing —or whether the latter habits caused it to frequently come into contact with the earthworms, which are always so plentiful in the rich black soils where mole-runs are most abundant, and so to select them as its principal because most easily obtained kind of food, at first seems difficult to say. A little reflection, however, induces us to believe that it was in hunting and following the earthworms that its engineering instincts were developed. And seeing that this mode of existence affords protection from numerous enemies above ground, which cannot reach it down below, we need not wonder that the Mole enjoys so extensive a geographical distribution, and is so numerous. Moreover, the peculiar rank odour diffused by its flesh appears to render it an unpalatable morsel to even hungry enemies; for no dog or cat will eat it, unless actually starving, and then they show every sign of disgust at the food.

The system of underground galleries, "runs," "fortresses,"&c., which the Mole constructs is very wonderful. Each animal has its own domain, or "encampment," as Professor Bell aptly terms it. The chief place is the "fortress," so called because of the circular tunnels around it, and the numerous short cuts by which these tunnels can be speedily approached from any side in case of danger. This important habitation is usually the object of much thought, and is selected if possible at the foot of some tree, or near a high bank. Thence radiate the underground "runs," which we may regard as the hunting-grounds of the Mole, its worm-preserves. These "runs" or galleries are continually being extended, either in search of food or water; for, like all gormandizers, especially carnivorous ones, the Mole is habitually thirsty. Its engineering invention not only enables it to extend its galleries to the neighbourhood of streams, but even to excavate pits or wells into which the rain-water can drain, so that it can depend on the supplies provided by its own ingenuity. The Mole is a hard worker. The pursuit of its food is at the expenditure of much physical energy, and so it is a voracious feeder. It follows the movements of the earthworm, as the North American Indians do those of the herds of wild buffaloes. When the rains have softened the soils, and the earthworms come near the surface, the Mole follows them like fate, and then excavates its runs so near the surface that we can trace them by the breaking in of the grassy roof.

Is there anything in the mere possession of land which makes animals quarrelsome? Land has been a fruitful source of wars among human kind in all generations, and of no small amount of litigation now that tribal wars are abolished in civilized countries. Among the lower animals the same spirit is exhibited. Each mole, for instance, has its own "domain" and worm-hunting ground. Should one mole trespass, in the ardour of its hunting instincts, or even impelled by hunger, on the territory of another, a cruel duel is the result; for the Mole is a most virulent enemy, and will attack its antagonist with a fury and tenacity we should not give the sleek-skinned animal credit for. When two moles meet in fight, whether for the favour of some female or to dispute possession of a hunting-ground, the battle rages so fiercely that not unfrequently it is continued on the surface of the ground, in spite of mutual danger. The victor nearly always turns cannibal, tearing its defeated foe in malicious triumph, and burying its long snout in the quivering entrails, as if sucking its enemy's blood were the crowning reward of successful valour.

The chief underground galleries and "runs" of the Moles are so well trodden that Professor Bell speaks of them as "highways." The rapidity with which the creatures move to and fro in these subterranean retreats is truly marvellous; for, at the slightest announcement of danger, they dart away from the points where it is threatened nearly as fast as a horse can trot. To dig a mole out of its burrows, therefore, is no slight task, and in the Eastern Counties it requires men who have specially devoted themselves to mole-catching as a profession, in order to fully understand the animal's underground movements and habits. So wily is the creature that, when these men have baited their traps, they have to rub the parts they have handled with a dead mole, in order to efface the smell which it would otherwise immediately detect. In the rich loamy meadows we may see the bent sticks set as traps over the "fortress"; or behold the trophies of the mole-catcher's victories slung from the branches of an adjoining tree, to indicate to the farmer that he has carried out his contract. The breeding-place of the female is not in the "fortress," but in mounds raised for the purpose, and lined with leaves, etc.

Mr. Dallas speaks as follows of the pairing instincts of this interesting creature :—" Very early in the year the Mole feels strange emotions stirring within him, and then he goes off gallantly, in his velvet coat, in search of a partner in his lonely encampment. That he will not be allowed to bring home his bride without many an appeal to his weapons is almost a matter of necessity, for by some singular dispensation the number of male moles is very much greater than that of the opposite sex, a disproportion which, as might be expected, gives rise to a good deal of jealousy and its natural consequences among such fierce and untamed spirits. As the Mole goes on his wooing he makes numerous but very shallow tracks in all directions. These have received the elegant name of *traces d'amour* from the French naturalists. The lady having been found, the next business is to secure possession of her, and this is attended with considerable difficulties, both from the impertinent intrusions of other males, and from a tendency on the part of the lady herself to run away from the proffered happiness. The intending bridegroom must have rather a hard time of it. But at length the bride's coyness and the assiduities of rivals are got rid of, and the pair settle down to inhabit, for a time, the same encampment, and to bring up their little family." It would appear that the affection of the male for his mate is of a very warm kind, for instances have been known of females being found in traps, with their devoted males lying dead beside them. Moreover, it is stated by good authorities that on occasions when their nest has been invaded by some sudden flood, both male and female have been seen struggling bravely and risking their own lives in order to save their helpless young.

The Mole has a tolerably high geological antiquity, for the fossil remains of one species (*Palæospalax magnus*), as large as a hedgehog, have been found in the Norfolk forest-bed, a formation which is geologically older than the Great Ice age. Fossil remains of allied species have also been found abundantly in the Miocene strata of France; but in all these cases the identification has been based on the peculiar character of the teeth and jaws. To know for certain whether the *Palæospalax* of the Norfolk forest-bed was an underground animal, we should require to examine the breast-bones, and those of the forelegs. These would at once enable us to decide whether it had acquired any or all of the subterranean habits which we have briefly sketched as distinguishing the common Mole.

Nearly allied to the Mole in many respects, but chiefly in their dentition, and therefore food, are those well-known and much maligned animals the SHREWS. Their habits are perhaps not so subterranean as those of the Moles, and in one instance we have a special adaptation to a semi-aquatic life. Still, all the species are burrowers, and one digs away galleries after the fashion of its relative. The common Shrew (*Sorex vulgaris*) is undoubtedly better known than even the Mole, for it is more frequently met with in country lanes. The only exception to its mouse-like shape is in the long taper snout, which at once indicates its relationship to the Moles, and the fact that it is intended to be an underground feeder.

Its dietary is purely insectivorous—worms, slugs, larvæ of beetles, and insects being all greedily devoured. Like its kinsman the Mole, it is very pugnacious, and two males rarely meet without a fight, which is usually to the death. Then follows the cannibalistic repast of the victor upon his fallen foe. The subterranean galleries which the Shrew excavates serve it both for worm and grub-hunting grounds and a home. Its taper snout here becomes a most useful plough in the soft and yielding soil, and at the same time enables it to root out its prey from their hiding-places.

Many natural history writers have noted the singular fact, well known to all dwellers in the country, that about autumn-time great numbers of dead shrews are found lying above ground, as if they were the victims of some annual epidemic. And it has been suggested, that as shrews are exceedingly voracious animals, and cannot subsist long without feeding, this sudden death may be due to starvation, as the worms generally sink down lower in the earth than usual during the dry months for the sake of moisture. The Shrews lack the powerful digging-limbs of the Moles, and therefore cannot follow them downwards; for their only or chief burrowing implement is their long, taper snout. It seems strange, however, that such annual destruction of shrew life should constantly occur. Those who regard "natural selection" as an actual law, would argue that the annual famines would ultimately have been provided against by the survivors, and the danger have been met. A little more observation is required to clear up the mysteries of these autumn visitations.

May they not be due to actual epidemics, brought on perhaps by lowered nutrition, due to decrease in their food supplies? It would be an interesting study on the part of any country naturalist to microscopically examine the blood and stomachs of some of these dead shrews, with a view to discovering the actual causes of death.

Perhaps there is not a creature in all our British fauna which has been more maligned than the pretty and harmless little Shrew. Its history in this respect plainly shows us what a savage and cruel thing ignorance is. Genuine humanity and kindness towards the lower animals have been developed in proportion as the habits and general natural history of those very creatures have been studied. Interest in them thus supplants prejudices against them. We soon find out how little we have understood them. In many cases we learn that we have been persecuting our own friends, and then self-interest impels us to desist. In other instances we learn to love them, as fellow-creatures sharing the same Divine compassion and care! And this latter is the right feeling,

> "For the great God who loveth us,
> He made and loveth all."

There is no need for us to dwell upon the injury which even the unconscious infliction of pain and cruelty exercised upon the lower animals reflects on man himself. It stunts the growth of the finer feelings of his nature, and develops those of intense selfishness. Whereas a kindly love of animals, an interest taken in the habits and ways of every object that enjoys the breath of life, will lift a man outside himself, and allow him to note the true relationships of the animal creation.

Even to this very day, in the more distant and less opened-out parts of the country, the Shrew is regarded with mistrust and actual dread. The most absurd malpractices are alleged against it, and in not a few places it is killed without mercy. The time is not very distant when this ignorant superstition was believed in by all people, even by those professing themselves educated beyond the common. Thus we find a clergyman named Topsell, in a book written in 1658 on "Four-footed Beasts," speaking of the Shrew as follows:—"It is a roving beast, feigning itself gentle and tame, but being touched, it biteth deep, and poyseneth deadly. It beareth a cruel minde, desiring to hurt anything, neither is there any creature that it loveth, or it loveth him, because it is feared of all. . . . They go very slowly; they are fraudulent, and take their prey by deceit. Many times they gnaw the oxes' hoofs in the stable"—and so on!

Poor little Shrew, whose savagest bite will not endow it with strength enough to break the skin of the human hand! But it was further reported concerning it, that if it walked over the limbs of reposing cattle, they would be smitten with paralysis. Moreover, even men and women and children could be "shrew-struck," whatever that vague terror might imply in those days of supposed witchcraft. Children were particularly liable to this malady, perhaps because they could not speak and tell what ailed them. But the remedies for these evils were as false as themselves, and frequently implied acts of cruelty from which, we are thankful to say, most people would now shrink. The chief cure for a "shrew-stroke" was to catch a living shrew, and place it in a hole which had been bored in an ash-tree specially for its reception. The hole was then plugged, and the creature allowed to die of starvation. "Shrew-ashes," as these trees were called, are still pointed out in some country places. Another remedy for the supposed "poysonous bite" of this animal was to get a shrew, burn it, and mix it with grease into an ointment wherewith to anoint the affected or "bitten" part. This, Topsell tells us, "doth bring a wonderful and most admirable cure and remedy." To monopolize such a remedy solely for shrew-bites hardly seemed logical, and so we find it, under another form, extended to the healing of bites of other animals. Thus we are informed that "the tail of a shrew being cut off and burned, and afterwards beaten into dust, and applied or anointed upon the sore of any man, which came by the bite of a greedy and ravenous dog, will in very short space make them both whole and sound, *so that the tail be cut off from the Shrew when she is alive*, and not dead, for then it have neither good operation nor efficacy in it." The Rev. J. G. Wood very pertinently suggests that this association by bad observers of the Shrew with cattle might be caused by the little animals visiting them for the sake of the insects which abound around them, and possibly torment them.

Another genus of Shrews is that called by naturalists *Crassopus fodiens*, but better known to anglers, and those who have wandered by river and brook-sides, by the name of the Water-Shrew. Like its terrestrial namesake, it has the peculiar pointed snout of burrowing animals, and, indeed, for a long time it was believed to be identical with the former animal. But we know it now to be both generically and specifically distinct. Its fringed tail and feet proclaim its aquatic habits, for the fringe enables the feet to act as oars, and the tail to be used as a rudder. The Water-Shrew is more abundant along the banks of streams in hilly districts than in plains, although it is not rare in the latter localities. Perhaps the reason it prefers rapidly-running streams is because the bottoms there are sandier and more free from mud, and also because underneath the stones and pebbles lie the insect larvæ and crustaceans which serve it for food. It does not restrict itself to the water-side, however, for it often wanders about the fields in search of worms, grubs, and insects. Still, it appears to enjoy an aquatic existence, and we have seen that by the peculiarity of its feet and tail it is evidently adapted for the habitat it prefers. It is an excellent diver, and loves to submerge its pretty little body beneath the water. The short, silken fur, dark on the back and nearly pure white on the belly, has the power of entangling a film of air, which keeps the water from damping the skin, so that the Water-Shrew when submerged appears as if coated with a thin layer of beady quicksilver. Other aquatic animals possess this habit, notably the large water-spider (*Argyroneta*).

Although so largely aquatic, the Water-Vole is nevertheless an underground dweller. It burrows galleries in the banks of the streams it frequents, and is wise enough to have several openings, in case of danger or attack, and always to have one which is beneath the water. It can thus gain admission to or exit from its subterranean dwelling either by land or water, and it is evident that such a sagacious arrangement must be an advantage to the contriver. It is a frisky, joyous little animal, and in early May it is most interesting to see the male and female chasing each other through the water, feigning attack and pursuit, and sometimes performing all the mimicry of war.

Although the character of its teeth shows us that the Water-Shrew is insectivorous, it does not refuse other diet. Small fish, tadpoles, and young frogs all contribute to its larder, and it can even make a hearty meal of such dead carcases as the streams may wash down. We are afraid, also, that it is not altogether innocent of devouring fish-spawn, and, what is worse, this habit has caused the innocent Water-Vole (*Arvicola amphibius*) to be included in the list of offenders in this respect. Mr. Wood draws attention to one very striking adaptation to its semi-aquatic life which the Water-Shrew possesses. Its ears are peculiarly formed, "so that as soon as the animal is wholly submerged the pressure of the water acts upon three small valves, which fold together, and effectually prevent the entrance of a single drop of water into the cavity of the ear. As soon as the animal rises from the water the pressure is removed, and the ears unfold like the petals of a flower when the sun shines warmly upon them."

The differences in the colour and fur of some varieties of Water-Shrews have caused naturalists to believe that another species exists, to which the name of *Sorex remifer* has been given. But intermediate varieties between this and the common Water-Shrew have proved that the former is the same species. A good deal of the differences in the coloration of fur depends upon the seasons, and the ages of individuals.

Popular zoology, which never aims at being accurate, groups all the animals we are now considering under the rough-and-ready term of "Rats and Mice." We have now to notice another group of underground dwellers, which belong to a different order. Their dentition shows us this at once, for their teeth do not interlock, as is the case with insectivorous animals, and the jaws are fashioned to work to and fro, after the fashion we call gnawing or nibbling; hence the name of *Rodentia* which is given to this order. It includes animals of various sizes and habits, from the Beaver to the Voles. The latter, like the Shrews, are of two kinds, one of them affecting semi-aquatic habits, and the other terrestrial; but being rodents, their food is almost exclusively vegetable in its character. Both are extensive burrowers, but the Field-Vole (*Arvicola agrestis*) is peculiarly so. It is its love for the sprouting seed-corn which causes it to burrow underneath newly-sown fields, where its subterranean galleries are visible on the surface by the long furrows it casts up. Mr. Bell tells us that the Field-Vole will also take possession of the empty burrows of other animals, particularly of those of the Mole. For a winter residence it usually selects wheat-ricks and barns, where it continues its depredations. Altogether, therefore, the Field-Vole is one of the greatest enemies the farmer has to contend against. The increase of late years of this and other similar animals seems to be due to the great destruction of our birds of prey, notably of the owls, which would otherwise keep them down, and prevent their undue increase. The late Mr. Edward Newman used to say that every owl was worth £5 a year to the British nation, on account of its usefulness in destroying animals of this character, whose prolific fertility would soon multiply them to such a degree that they would soon overrun a country. At the late meeting of the British Association in Dublin, Sir Walter Elliott made some observations on the annual increase of the Field-Vole of late years. In the spring of 1876 they appeared in such numbers in the hill pasture-farms of the border districts between England and Scotland as to destroy the grazing ground on which the sheep depended in spring, thus causing serious loss to the farmers by the impoverishment and death of their stock. The shepherds destroyed as many as they could, but without sensibly diminishing their numbers, although they were assisted by birds and beasts of prey, hawks, owls, buzzards, weasels, foxes, etc. At the same time that the Field-Vole was doing such mischief along the borders, another species (*Arvicola arvalis*), not known in England, made its appearance in Hungary, and attacked the cornfields there. This it had done to a less degree two or three years before, and in 1877 they attacked the wheat-fields of Moldavia. The Field-Voles do not restrict their ravages to newly-sown fields or to green pastures; they also attack plantations of young trees, and do much harm through nibbling the roots and shoots of living trees and shrubs. They burrow beneath the ground, and there find in such plantations food ready to their taste. The young woods then droop and wither as if blighted, and none but those in the secret know of the subterranean enemy which has caused all the mischief. Mr. Jesse, in his "Gleanings," has put on record the great damage which the Field-Voles did to the new plantations in Dean Forest and the New Forest. He states that the roots of the trees were always eaten through whenever they obstructed the "runs" of the Voles; but it should be remembered that these very "runs" are excavated in order that the burrowers may find vegetable food. Mr. Jesse tells us that pits were dug, in order that the Voles might fall therein, and this mode of capture proved so successful that thousands were caught. What with this and other methods of destruction, he calculates that no fewer than two hundred thousand voles were slain in the plantations of the two above-mentioned forests.

In the paper just referred to Sir Walter Elliott expressed his opinion that it was worth the consideration of game-preservers as to whether hawks, owls, weasels, etc., should be so greatly exterminated as they are by ignorant gamekeepers. For ourselves we would speak more emphatically on this point. Even from the sportsman's point of view the matter is worth careful consideration. Our winged game has deteriorated so much in its powers of flight, for want of birds of prey picking out the worst, that sportsmen complain of the insipidity of the field. We hear and read of chronic epidemics taking off such myriads of grouse and partridges that sometimes few are left to the gun. The fact is, when nature was allowed to keep up her police in the shape of birds and beasts of prey, the weakly were thinned off, and none but the strong left to perpetuate the race. But since we stepped in, and in our greediness to raise as many "birds" as possible, have indiscriminately massacred their natural enemies, we have in reality protected the weakly, allowed them to breed, and so deteriorated the race. Neither the species we have sought to protect, the birds of prey, nor the sportsmen have been gainers by the disturbance of the natural balance. We have succeeded in raising a race of weakly birds, which cold, mildew, or internal parasitical worms, such as "gapes," carry off by thousands. Moles and hedgehogs, which are the natural enemies of the Vole, by devouring the food which would otherwise cause the Voles to multiply, are destroyed most ruthlessly, and by professional slayers; whereas the Voles, greatly more destructive to crops and young trees, are allowed to increase unchecked, until some such panic occurs as that which recently alarmed the Border farmers.

We have a good deal more sympathy for the Water-Vole (*Arvicola amphibius*). In the first place, it has constantly to suffer for the faults of other animals, and a false accusation is sure to beget sympathy for the accused in the heart of every Englishman. It usually goes by the name of the "Water-Rat," and so all the sins of that heinous offender are laid on the head of the poor Water-Vole. It is an unfortunate thing for the latter animal that it so much resembles the former in general appearance. The true brown rat will visit river-banks and devour fish wherever it can obtain them; but the Water-Vole is a pure vegetarian, as its teeth plainly indicate. It feeds on aquatic plants, their stems, leaves, or seeds; the common mare's tail (*Equisetum*) being evidently a favourite morsel with it, notwithstanding its flinty skin. Mr. Wood says he has often seen it feeding on the bark of the common rush. Now, neither of these plants contains much nourishment, and therefore we think it is highly probable that the Water-Vole only resorts to them because of their silicious cuticles, gnawing which enables it to keep down the too rapid growth of its incisor teeth. Many animals gnaw at substances for this purpose, and it is easily conceivable that the Water-Vole, whose vegetable diet is of so succulent a character generally, must require dental practice of such a kind. In many respects the Water-Vole is nearly allied to the Beaver. It is one of the commonest of our British mammals, and may be found along the banks of most clear streams. The numerous holes which the observer beholds in these banks are due to the tunnelling propensities of the Water-Vole. It excavates in the soft alluvial soil of the banks, and forms galleries of some length, which serve it both as a home and special breeding-place. We may therefore consider it as an underground dweller, for it seeks in the bosom of mother earth that shelter which would perhaps be denied it above ground. It has been complained, and perhaps with some reason, that the Water-Vole does harm by weakening the banks of rivers by the numerous tunnels it makes. This may be true, but the Vole might allege in defence that it is obliged to live somewhere!

We are glad to add our testimony to that of numerous other observers as to the harmless character of the Water-Vole. There is not the slightest foundation for the accusations against it of destroying fish, fish-spawn or young, or young ducks. For such offences the brown rat ought to be indicted, not the Water-Vole. When aquatic vegetation is scanty, it will wander inland, and devour garden produce, but this is very rarely. To a careless observer, its short snub nose will readily distinguish it, even at a glance, from the brown rat.

Turn we now to another rodent, the very type of harmlessness in itself, timid, shy, and yet one of the greatest enemies the industrious farmer has to cope with. We allude to the RABBIT (*Lepus cuniculus*). To see it in its jubilant and yet fearsome innocence, you must get to some gorse-covered heath towards evening of a summer's day. Observe how they gambol in the most erratic and fantastic fashion—now stampeding for a score of yards as if chased by their bitterest enemies, and then suddenly stopping to nibble at some favourite herb; perhaps to divert and double again towards the point whence they originally started. The whole group, scattered over the naked part of the heath, then perhaps breaks up into frolicsome twos or threes, which chase each other into their holes. The males endeavour to belie their harmless appearance by stamping the ground angrily with their hind feet, but their timid neighbours are evidently too much accustomed to this innocent fiction to let it frighten them. Poor gambolling creatures, there are few animals which have a larger host of varied enemies than they! Hawk, eagle, owl, fox, dog, weasel, and even man, delight in their destruction; and yet these persecuted creatures, so burdened with the care and fear of a hunted life, give themselves up to enjoyments perhaps fuller of real fun and genuine humour than those indulged in by any other animals!

That the Rabbit is an underground dweller every one is aware. Its excavations are visible on every sandy warren, and its irregular burrows communicate with each other below the soil like the streets of a large town. Besides these we have the *extraordinary* burrows, dug by the female rabbits as nurseries. At the further ends of these secure retreats a large quantity of dried grass is laid, and this is covered over or intermixed with the soft fur from the Rabbit's breast, so as to form the warm and comfortable nest which will receive the seven or eight blind, naked, and utterly helpless young. Their reproductive powers are extraordinarily great, so much so that if they were not kept down by their numerous enemies, they would speedily overrun every county and eat up its vegetation. No place seems unfit for their development, if the soil is not too stiff or rocky to forbid their excavating their burrows. The few rabbits taken over to Australia, perhaps more as curiosities or home-pets than anything else, threaten to become one of the greatest plagues the colonists have to deal with, for there is an absence of those natural foes which abound in Great Britain. And yet a good rabbit warren, especially if it breed a peculiar colour, such as the gray rabbits on Brandon Heath, in Suffolk, is perhaps one of the most profitable of undertakings. They are animals which always find a market, for their flesh is the food of the people. Their furs are valuable, and capable of being manipulated into the semblance of those deemed more costly; and many a lady who is perhaps treasuring her furs as real sable or ermine, is little aware that " rabbits " have contributed the main portion of the compound!

Unfortunately for its reputation with the farmer, the Rabbit is a very wasteful feeder. It destroys much more than it eats, nibbling a little bit here and there as if in sheer destructiveness, and gnawing away the bark of young trees. No wonder many farmers regard them as "ground vermin," and are, perhaps, only compensated for their wanton destructiveness by the few days rabbit-shooting accorded them by their landlords. The fact is, rabbits have no right to be encouraged where good farming is carried on. In such places they ought to be exterminated, and allowed to develop over those numerous waste lands whereon nothing else will live, but where the Rabbit finds an abundance of food and accommodation. In this way the rich soils would be freed from a troublesome enemy, and the barren unproductive land be able to contribute largely and profitably to the food-supplies of the country.

Of late years a hybrid race of rabbits, bred of a cross between the Hare and the Rabbit, has been successfully cultivated. These hybrids, singularly enough, and unlike the general rule of hybridization, are able to breed among themselves. The name of *Lepus Darwinii* has been given to this remarkable zoological manufacture of a new species. In Heligo-

THE RABBIT (*Lepus cuniculus*).

land this kind of rabbit is bred specially for the markets, where it is in high request, and its flesh partakes alike of the best qualities of that of the Hare and of the common Rabbit.

Few people would think that lingering about the

entrances of the rabbit burrows there are certain parasites which threaten to avenge the persecutions of the dog and the fox on these innocent creatures; and yet such is the case. That well-known insect the dog-tick (*Ixodes ricinus*), or rather the female, haunts these localities, and fastens itself on the first dog or fox which thrusts its nose in the mouth of the tempting burrow. These dog-ticks may nearly always be found in such situations. After once they have established themselves on their new hosts, they propagate their kind at the expense of its ¦comfort, not unfrequently causing it much suffering. Rabbits are also liable to a disease, caused by an internal parasite, which, singularly enough, never advances within their bodies beyond the stage in which we there always find it. But should a dog, fox, or wolf devour such a suffering rabbit, then the parasite is transferred to the stomach of the devourer. There it undergoes a marvellous change, advancing beyond the stage in which we knew it in the Rabbit, and taking up a different position in the body of its second host. It is now the well-known tapeworm of the dog, and attaches itself by means of hooks and suckers to the mucous membrane of the intestines.

One almost naturally associates the name of one underground dweller with another, the Fox with the Rabbit. Yet what a difference in their habits and natures! One the very type of animal innocence, the other of carnivorous cunning and cruelty; and still there are some traits in the character of the Fox which are admirable. Its devotion to its young and courage manifested in their defence are well known; and if a cub be taken young, we have known it to become almost as much attached to its master as a dog. All its good qualities, however, are completely absorbed in its proverbial cunning. The traditions of all peoples, wherever the Fox is found, have expressed this fact; and some of the oldest fables in the old and new worlds make the Fox their central figure.

Can we forget that He "who had not where to lay His head," adverted to the underground habits of this animal? "The Foxes have holes," all the world over, whatever species we may select, not even excepting the Arctic Fox, which will burrow in the snow. Like many of the animals liable to pursuit, such as the Mole, Shrew, etc., the Fox has special tail-glands which secrete the strong odour which characterizes them. In the Fox, however, it is this odour which the hounds take up and follow, and at certain times of the year it appears to be very strong, insomuch that we can easily tell for ourselves if a fox have crossed the path a short time previously. The Fox seems to be well aware of the dangerous consequences to itself of this tell-tale scent, and hence the numerous dodges it resorts to to throw the pursuing dogs off it. It will return on its former track, or "double," as it is called, and then make most extraordinary leaps so as to throw the hounds off. Nay, Mr. Wood tells us that it is sagacious enough even to perfume itself with any odorous substance it may come across, in order to deceive the keen-scented dogs. It is questionable, however, whether we have not an instance here of a change which has taken place in the utility of a secretion. The Fox originally had this secreting power given to it either for sexual purposes, so that male might find female ; or, perhaps, even to disgust its natural enemies with the taste of its flesh. Except just at the moment of its death, when their passions are excited, dogs even now will not touch the flesh of the Fox. And this nauseating odour may therefore have been largely protective. But now, alas for the Fox, man has appeared upon the scene, and in his love of sport has taken advantage of that very scent (which may have been intended to repel the Fox's enemies), to track and hunt the creature to its death!

The "holes" or burrows of the Fox are scooped out of the earth by means of the animal's strong digging paws. It exhibits much craft and cunning in excavating these holes, carrying the galleries in and out of the roots of some large tree, or, in rocky ground, in and between the interstices of the stones. But it shirks such labour whenever possible, and will take possession of and utilize the holes of the Badger and Rabbit when it can. These underground retreats are well known to sportsmen by the name of "earths." The Fox usually remains concealed in them during the day, and issues thence at night on its destructive foraging expeditions. No animal seems more instinctively aware that it has very cunning enemies to deal with. Its own craftiness seems to make it suspicious of every creature except those on which it preys. Hence the sagacious suspicion with which it examines the mouth of its hole on its return from a journey. Anything of the nature of a trap or a gin is scented at once, and tales of the most remarkable sagacity are related by trustworthy observers of the various ways in which the Fox has defeated all such attempts at its capture. Similarly, before leaving its burrow, its first care is to examine the neighbourhood of the mouth, to see that no snare has been laid. A French naturalist relates that a fox has been known to remain within its retreat without food for fifteen days, rather than risk the danger of falling into a trap which it suspected had been set for it. The Fox lives as long as fourteen years, and if the country be much "hunted," we may depend on it that by the time it has reached such an age, its stock of cunning must be very large.

It is with pleasure that we have the opportunity of saying a good word for another much-maligned and much-persecuted creature, the BADGER (*Meles taxus*). Fortunately a humaner law has taken this poor creature under its protection, and so "Badger-baiting," as the "sport" of tormenting the poor thing was called, is now illegal. It is a sad reflection that the indulgence in that brutal cruelty which comes of thoughtlessness rather than from a desire to inflict pain, should have at length enriched the English language with an additional verb! "To badger" is now used legitimately to signify a persistent endeavour to annoy and worry. What an amount of cruelty is represented by this circumstance! The result of this "badgering" persecution is that the animal whose sufferings have given us the word is now all but extinct in Great Britain.

And yet we question whether there is any member of our English fauna in reality more truly harmless.

Left alone, it is thoroughly inoffensive, although its strength of jaws and claws makes it a formidable enemy when it is worried up to that pitch of self-defence at which even a worm would turn. In former

THE BADGER (*Meles taxus*).

times the Badger was placed in a tub, and then continuously worried by dogs, until the "amusement" not unfrequently ended in both dogs and Badger suffering to the death.

As an underground dweller, the Badger is most admirably adapted to that mode of life; and its long, taper, powerful snout, and strong digging claws are equally good tools wherewith to excavate its subterranean dwelling-place. Like its near relation the Bear, it is *plantigrade*—that is to say, the whole foot is placed upon the ground at every stride. This makes it a slow and somewhat clumsy walker, just as the Bear is; but these strong feet are of capital use to the animal when burrowing. Its claws are peculiarly curved, and strong, and the short feet which they terminate must be very capital digging implements. When engaged in excavating its burrow, the Badger uses its snout to push the earth aside with, and mean time the forefeet are engaged in digging, whilst the hind feet are used to throw the earth to the rear as much as possible. A good deal of pains and care are taken to remove the excavated earth from near the hole, and, as the Badger is a large animal, and therefore requires a capacious burrow, there must be a very large quantity of *débris* to be thus disposed of. When its underground abode is thus contrived, the Badger, like the Rabbit, proceeds to prepare one part of it for the especial purpose of a nursery. There the female makes her comfortable nest, generally of well-dried grass, which must be a warm and snug retreat for her three or four young when these are born. Nor has it been neglected to stock this subterranean home with necessary provisions, in the shape of well-rolled balls of grass, etc. The situation chosen for these burrows is generally in the gloomy depth of some wood, or the coppice-planted side of a hill. The entrance to the burrow is usually steep and tortuous, and the underground home has often more than one apartment in case of danger. In these days, when the "sewage nuisance" is occupying public attention, and sanitary science seems helpless to deal with an increasing difficulty, the devices of the Badger to provide for the removal of ordure, etc., within his subterranean retreat are worth a remark. It digs ingeniously-designed sinks or pits, and in these all the offensive refuse and fæces are thrown and covered up, and thus the cleanly animal takes due care that its dark and gloomy home shall at any rate be clean! The odour which the Badgers, male and female, themselves evolve is, as usual, secreted by special tail-glands, and this enables the male and female animals to obtain traces of each other—a contrivance all the more necessary as Badgers are never numerically abundant, and must frequently roam about at great distances from each other. It is this fetid secretion which has obtained for the Badger its Scotch name of the "Stinking Brock"—*broc* being its ancient Anglo-Saxon name.

In addition to its vegetable diet of grass, roots, earth-nuts, beech-mast, etc., the Badger will occasionally vary its diet with insect and animal food. It is very fond of wasp-grubs, and does a great deal of good in digging out wasp-nests from the banks—a feat for which its powerful curved claws admirably adapt it. Its tough hide and dense, coarse hair, meantime completely protect it from the stings of the enraged wasps, which cling to it and buzz about it in vain, as it destroys both their home and their offspring.

It will be thus seen that the Badger is about as inoffensive in itself, and as harmless to man, as any of our native wild animals can be. There is a popular notion about it that it is a dull and stupid creature, stubborn and sulky. But the almost fox-like sagacity with which it scents traps and snares, and the means it adopts to subvert them, at once prove that it is anything but "stupid." And the ease with which it can be tamed, and the affection it displays for those who care for it, equally attest its pliant disposition. Professor Bell himself gives us the following account of a young badger he had tamed; or, rather, the animal had been purchased from a cottager with whose children it had been seen playing as familiarly as a puppy. Professor Bell tells us that he "found the animal had been taken when very young, and had been brought up as a playmate of the children; it had, however, become rather rough in its fondness, and the poor man was willing to part with it. It thus came into my possession, and soon became a great favourite, showing, too, on its part, great attachment to me and the household. He followed me like a dog, yelping and barking with a peculiar sharp cry when he found himself shut out of the room in which I happened to be sitting. He was accustomed to come into our dining-room during dinner, of which he was generally permitted to partake, and he always ate his morsels in a very orderly manner. He was, in fact, an affectionate, gentle, good-tempered fellow, and very cleanly withal." That is our opinion of the Badger, wild or tame; and we hope that the spirit of humanity which the modern love of natural history is so powerfully helping to develop, and which has already borne good fruit in the protection extended during their "close time" to most of our wild birds, will ere long protect our native mammalia from that indiscriminate slaughter which harms by brutalizing those who indulge in it, even more than the poor creatures that are hunted to extinction!

We have several other native mammals which occasionally resort to underground retreats, although none are at the special labour and trouble of excavating them. The Otter (*Lutra vulgaris*) will occasionally excavate a kind of hollow in the softer parts of the river banks which it frequents; but it prefers some deserted burrow, or natural hole or crevice, to any contrivance of its own, which latter, at the best, is a very sorry piece of work. The natural hollow beneath the overhanging roots of a tree is one of its favourite haunts, and here it usually brings up its young, to which it is devoted almost beyond any other of our wild animals. Our Brown and Black Rats, also, although neither species is purely indigenous, pass a good deal of their lives underground, where they prefer to have their "runs" in the neighbourhood of houses and buildings, and generally beneath the very floors. The Black Rat (*Mus rattus*), commonly called the "Old English Rat," is now nearly extinct in this country, having been driven out of its old haunts by the Brown, or Norway Rat (*Mus decumanus*), just as the aboriginal Britons were replaced by the ancient Anglo-Saxon conquerors and settlers. Before the Norway Rat came into this country, the Black Rat was quite as plentiful as the former now is. Its name serves to show us how long the *black* species has been acclimatized with us, but he is only a foreigner after all, and was probably imported into England from France. Some of our species of *Mice* also occasionally resort to holes underground, although they usually occupy such subterranean " runs " as they find, rather than construct them. The Harvest Mouse (*Mus messorius*) resorts to subterranean burrows during the winter months, and there hybernates. The Field Mouse (*Mus sylvaticus*) has also underground retreats, where, unfortunately for us, it lays up much store of grain for winter use. These subterranean abodes are usually in natural excavations under the roots of trees. Pennant says that it is in quest of these hidden hoards of food made by the Field Mouse that the hog does so much harm by rooting up the ground. The Common Marten (*Martes foina*), Polecat (*Mustela putorius*), and Weasel (*Mustela vulgaris*), also frequently use holes and crevices in the ground for their protection; and the Ermine (*Mustela erminea*) has been known to utilize the deserted underground galleries and citadels of the common Mole.

Nor should we omit reference to the fact that some of the "birds of the air" are fain to seek abodes underground. Among the most indefatigable of burrowers in this respect is the Sand Martin (*Hirundo riparia*), which exhibits great skill in the way with which it excavates its tunnel in the face of a sandy cliff. The Kingfisher also digs out a hollow for its nest, if it cannot find one to its hand. The Puffin prefers to rob the Rabbit of its burrow, but if it cannot do so it will hollow one out for itself. For timid although the wild Rabbit be, it does not give up its subterranean home obtained at the expense of so much labour, without contention; and many comical combats take place before the Puffin finally vanquishes it. Jackdaws, Stockdoves, Sheldrakes, and other British birds, also seek for nest-shelter in underground retreats; whilst the Stormy Petrel digs out a most elaborate tunnel, leading to a capacious cell, from the blown sandbanks along the coasts it frequents.

Enough has been said, however, to indicate that the soil beneath us affords its convenient shelter to many vertebrate animals, just as the waters of our seas and rivers do to the species equally adapted to an aquatic existence. Modern science has brought into greater prominence than ever that wonderful doctrine of adaptation of animal and vegetable life to its surroundings which, in our opinion, is one of the strongest evidences supplied by natural religion of the constant superintendence of a Personal and Intelligent Being.

CHAPTER III.

INVERTEBRATE DWELLERS UNDERGROUND.

The complex organization of warm-blooded or vertebrate animals renders it impossible for many of them to live under conditions which are more favourable to creatures simpler in structure and habit. Hence we find a much larger number of invertebrate animals living underground than of the higher group. The periods during which they lead this subterranean existence are varied. Some of the animals, as the Mole-Cricket, Earth-worm, etc., cannot habitually live elsewhere; others adopt the habit periodically or occasionally. Of the most notable of these underground species we purpose now taking notice. We shall find much to learn from some of them, and perhaps be astonished that we need not go to Herculaneum or Pompeii to find buried cities, for they occur beneath our own feet. And although they be cities or communities of *insects*, instead of *men*, the interest created by these underground habitations increases the more we study them.

Let us turn our attention first to those animals whose peculiar anatomy indicates their special adaptation to an underground existence. Next to the Mole, the Mole-Cricket (*Gryllotalpa vulgaris*) is perhaps one of the most admirably fitted for the life it leads beneath the soil. Although an invertebrate animal (whilst the true mole is vertebrate), one cannot but be surprised at the similarity of the plan on which the fore-limbs of these two creatures—separated by so wide a zoological division—have been fashioned. Popular observation has long noticed this fact; hence the English name of the insect. Its build at once shows us what a muscular creature it is, in spite of its lightness of weight. Notwithstanding the strong resemblance in every part and detail of the first pair of

THE MOLE-CRICKET (*Gryllotalpa vulgaris*).

legs in the Mole-Cricket to those of the Mole, the likeness is only the result of modifying *two* different sets of animal limbs to *one* kind of work. We have the same principle exemplified in the pectoral fins of fish and the paddles of the Whale or Dolphin—in the wings of the bird and those of the bat.

We kept some mole-crickets obtained from a rich loamy field at Beccles, in Suffolk, for a long time. It was quite amusing to observe how they used their front legs for burrowing, exactly after the manner of the Mole—certainly the resemblance was quite as striking as the method of swimming of fish is to that of cetaceans. They were domesticated in the soil of a flower-pot, and when placed on the surface, they disappeared beneath with the same kind of ghost-like motion that we noticed in the Moles. Like its structural prototype, the Mole-Cricket burrows underground, although it is rather herbivorous than carnivorous in its diet, so that it is anything but a welcome habitant in the market-gardens where it frequently takes up its abode. Whilst burrowing beneath the soil, it attacks the roots of all kinds of plants, so that the latter gradually die, and their decay will perhaps be assigned to "worms." Still the Mole-Cricket does not seem averse to insect food, especially worms, of which it is very fond, and devours a good many. Like all animals which are fond of fighting, it is occasionally a cannibal. This cannibal habit seems always to have been formed from revengeful feelings, rather than dearth of food. If two mole-crickets (especially two males) be placed in a box, the result will be an approximation to the melancholy end of the Kilkenny Cats! The stronger will be the victor; and, although he may have lost a limb or two in the fearful duel, he will inevitably feast upon his vanquished foe. Nay, it is on record that when a mole-cricket had been cut in two by a spade the forepart has been seen devouring its severed hinder part!

The male insect differs from the female in the position of the wing-covers, or *elytra*. In the former the right elytron wraps over the left, whereas in the female the left folds over the right. There is also a difference in the measures of the wings of the two sexes. The females appear to be the most abundantly represented, and they lay an immense number of eggs during the summer months. When hatched, the young remain underground, and during the winter repose in a dormant condition. They do not appear above the surface until they have undergone their changes of skin, or metamorphoses, and their wings have been fully grown. This does not take place until the succeeding summer, so that a newly-fledged mole-cricket is a year old. The eggs are usually deposited at so shallow a depth underground that the sun's heat can penetrate to them, and hatch them into life. The nest-burrows of the Mole-Cricket, therefore, are different from its ordinary subterranean tunnels, and are intended for a special purpose, which speaks much for the instinct of these singular insects. In its ordinary habits the Mole-Cricket constructs, like its namesake, a neatly-finished chamber, which is approached by winding galleries. Like the Mole, also, its course under ground may frequently be traced by the ridges of earth it throws up to the surface. The passages it forms are not sufficiently wide to allow the insect to turn about; but this difficulty is got over by the adroitness with which (thanks to the very sensitive bristles at the end of its body, which act like the antennæ in front) it can move backwards or forwards with equal ease.

These remarkable bristles also serve to communicate to their possessor warning of danger that may threaten it at the rear, when it is engaged in employing its powerful front legs in burrowing.

The possession of wings shows us plainly that the underground habits of the Mole-Cricket have been acquired. In proportion as its fore-limbs have been so remarkably modified and adapted for subterranean uses, its wings have lost their power of extensive flight, and are now so small in proportion to the size and weight of the insect's body, that they can only carry it in a series of dips or jerky flights. Sight, however, does not appear to have been much affected, possibly from the fact that in the summer months both males and females pass much time above ground, when the use of sight is constantly required. The male is said to be sometimes luminous, or phosphorescent; so that it has been mistaken, when flying at night, for the Will-o'-the-wisp.

Whilst speaking of the Mole-Cricket, we may as well here allude to the partially underground habits of its cousin, the FIELD-CRICKET (*Acheta campestris*). Although it resorts to subterranean shelter less than the former, still it makes use of the soil beneath us for protective purposes. It excavates burrows in banks where the soil is looser than usual, and here it lodges all day, only issuing forth at night, when it pipes its well-known shrilly notes. These underground burrows are excavated by the insects in a tortuous manner, and occasionally the observer may see them sitting within the entrances to their habitations even in the daytime, after the manner of Giant

Pope in the "Pilgrim's Progress." The Field-Cricket is an odd-tempered, irascible little creature, and allows its angry passions to get the better of its judgment. Hence it is an easy matter to draw it forth from the bottom of its hole by simply inserting

FIELD CRICKETS (*one emerging from its burrow*).

a long stalk of grass. The irritable insect fastens on the end at once, and foolishly suffers itself to be dragged out of its retreat rather than let go. As a rule, each field-cricket has a separate burrow, but this single-blessedness is only of diurnal practice, for, in the evening, the insects gather together at a general nocturnal meeting.

Nearly allied to the Field-Cricket is the beautiful GREEN GRASSHOPPER, so frequently to be seen on the dewy hedgerows in September. Its grass-green colour is a great protection to it, as every one must see at a glance. The long, formidable-looking organ at the end of the body is the ovipositor, and by its means the eggs of this insect can be laid on the ground, after the ovipositor has first acted as a boring instrument to dig a hole for their reception. Ten or twelve eggs are placed in one hole, and then another is bored, and this goes on until all the eggs are deposited. The eggs hatch in the ground, and at first are as small as a gnat's.

Mother Earth affords home and shelter for the living as well as for the dead. Many species of Bees and Wasps live in useful knowledge of the fact; but among them none more so than the now highly appreciated HUMBLE-BEE, well named by naturalists, on account of its underground habits, *Bombus terrestris*. Its English name is almost common property both with us and the Germans, the latter terming it *Hummel-Biene*. In both instances it is doubtless derived from the loud, humming sound made by this insect. Speaking personally, there are few British insects for which we have a greater respect than the Humble-Bee. It is the very type of a business-like body, attending only to its own affairs, more industrious even than the Ant, more devoted to its young than even the Spider. Its life, if not one of anxiety, is one of continual labour and care. By what singular arrangement is it that the Humble-Bees die off so strangely at the close of summer, but first depute, as it were, one or two of their number to *live!* This is actually the case. The male bees nearly always die, and generally only one or two of the females survive. These pass the cold months of winter in a state of torpidity, hiding away wherever they can obtain necessary shelter, but stimulated into active life by the reviving warmth of spring days. Then they issue forth to a new existence, seeking some loamy hedge-bank, where perhaps a field-mouse has burrowed a hole. Should the Humble-Bee be fortunate enough to meet with one, much labour of excavation will be saved to it. No small amount of surveying instinct is displayed in the spring, whilst these insects are looking for the proper soils and sites; and nothing can exceed the care taken lest they are watched during the process. Having finally fixed upon a suitable spot, the Humble-Bee sets to work to excavate a hollow in the earth to contain her nest. Her fore-legs loosen the soil, grain by grain, and transfer the particles to the middle legs, which in turn pass them on to the hind-legs, and the latter then push the earth as far away as possible. A winding gallery or tunnel, one or two feet long, is thus made wide enough to allow two bees to pass, and the further end is hollowed into a smaller chamber. This is lined with leaves, and then a few waxen cells are built for the young. The latter belong to the *Worker* class, and their first duties are to enlarge the chamber in which they were born, for the purpose of enabling it to receive other and more numerous occupants. When completed, the underground colony founded by the original female Humble-Bee consists of males, females (large and small kinds), and workers. The total number of colonists thus com-

CELLS OF THE HUMBLE-BEE.

posed, when the underground republic is complete, will range to about two hundred. Sometimes, how-

HUMBLE-BEES *supporting a brood comb.*

ever, it is much lower than this. The male and female humble-bees usually make their appearance late in the summer, by which time their elder worker brethren have enlarged the home sufficiently to properly house them. The female is the largest-sized of these insects, and the worker is the smallest. In shape, size, and colour-markings, we might readily mistake these three typical members of one underground commonwealth for so many distinct *species* of insects.. Late in autumn, as we have seen, all die off except the one or two females intended to perpetuate the race and to found a new colony the following year.

The Humble-Bee is one of the most useful of insects, as well as one of the most rational. Its visits to flowers must produce considerable crossing, on account of the ease with which the pollen-grains adhere to its hairy body. It is rational, because it has been observed, after endeavouring to penetrate to the interior of many exotic flowers to which it was unaccustomed (in order to get at the honey in the nectary), and found no way therein, to bite a hole in the corollas at their base, and thus get at the coveted sweets from the outside. Nay, there is sufficient reason to believe that this habit, once indulged in, is practised as a shorter method for obtaining honey generally. We may nearly always find the flowers of the Gorse and the Broom perforated by round holes, which the Humble-Bees have cut in this way. Moreover, the habit is not universal. Some Humble-Bees practise it more than others.

But of all useful plants to which the Humble-Bee is necessary, the common Red Clover is perhaps the most important. The flowers of this plant cannot fertilize themselves, and of all insects the common Humble-Bee and the Red-tailed Humble-Bee can cross them best. Clover grows splendidly in New Zealand, and is there a most useful crop; but it cannot produce seed, for New Zealand has no native Humble-Bees, and so the colonists have to send for fresh clover-seed every year to Europe at considerable expense. The attempt has therefore been made, but so far without success, to convey Humble-Bees to New Zealand for the purpose of there acclimatizing them with a view to crossing the clover flowers. There can be no doubt that ere long the dormant females will be carried over successfully, perhaps packed in moss and enclosed in an ice-chest, so that the heat of the equator, which has to be traversed, does not wake them up too soon. At any rate the attempted experiment is a plain proof of the importance which modern natural history has taught us to attach to the operations of these industrious little insects.

In the opinion of some naturalists, the Red-tipped Humble-Bee (*Bombus lapidarius*) is even more useful to clover fertilization than the common species above mentioned. It always goes to the natural openings of flowers, and does not surreptitiously snip out holes in order to get at the nectar from the outside. Having a longer proboscis, it is also enabled to get down to the bottom of flowers which the common Humble-Bee cannot reach. It is a more beautiful insect to look at than the latter, and derives its name from its habit of making its nest among heaps of stone, generally among the hillocks gathered for road-mending. It sometimes burrows in the ground, however, and makes its nest there. The females and the workers are coloured alike, but different in size; whilst the males are variable in colour, and are usually black.

In addition to the Bees which found underground colonies, such as those above mentioned, we have others preferring a solitary life under similar conditions, and some which are of intermediate habits. The genus *Andrena*, for instance, are well known for their use in crossing numerous wild flowers, and remarkable for their tunnelling abilities. Although these insects are small, they make considerable excavations. A colony of *Andrena* Bees makes the ground look as if riddled with holes, in and out of which the busy, pollen-covered insects are perpetually passing. These holes descend to as much as six or eight inches from the surface, and terminate in a rounded chamber, where the pollen is stored in the shape and size of a pea. All the work of excavating this subterranean storehouse falls to the lot of the females, for the males are unable to burrow on account of the weakness of their fore-legs.

Another genus of the British burrowing Bees is that known as *Eucera*. The males have very long antennæ and are very beautiful insects. But they deserve to rank low in insect civilization, if only for the manner with which they treat their females. Like savages and other men degraded in the scale of morality, the weaker sex is here made to bear the heaviest burdens. The deep burrows of the *Eucera*, generally made in a stiff, clayey soil, the oval bottom of which is beaten hard in order to enable it to store safely both honey and pollen, are all excavated by the female insects. In addition, they have also to keep the larder well filled after they have dug it out and prepared it; whilst the males hover about in lazy carelessness.

Mr. Wood tells us that the boldest of these British underground burrowers is a bee known by the name

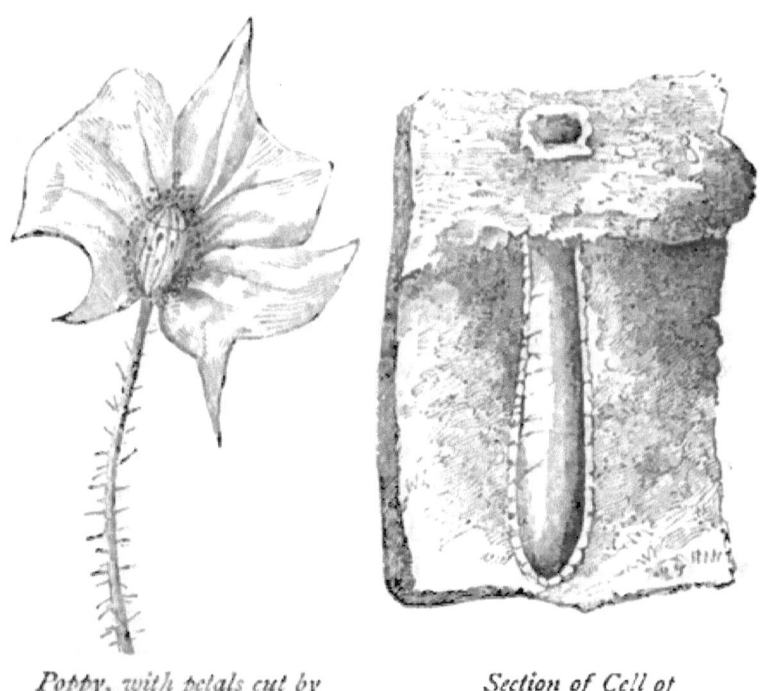

Poppy, with petals cut by TAPESTRY-BEE.   *Section of Cell of* TAPESTRY-BEE.

of *Philanthus triangulum*. It actually provisions its nest, after the latter has been excavated, with both Humble-Bees and Andrenas, which it will carry off bodily. Another genus of burrowing bees (*Cerceris*) stores its subterranean den with a variety of insect prey, including even hard beetles. As the latter prey on many which are injurious to vegetation, Cerceres are friends of the farmer, rather than foes, and should therefore be protected.

Lovers of gardens have no doubt noticed that the leaves of the Lilac and other plants, and especially such large-petalled flowers as those of the Poppy, frequently have almost circular pieces cut out of them. This is the work of the Tapestry Bee (*Osmia papaveris*), also an underground dweller; for it burrows holes in the ground to the depth of three inches, and lines them throughout with these fragments of leaves and flowers. The bottom of the burrow is hollowed out into a small chamber, in which the "bee-bread" and other food is stored, and herein its single egg is laid. The lower part is then neatly folded over with the remains of the vegetable tapestry, and the upper part of the burrow filled in with earth. The hard paths in our cornfields seem to be favourable sites with the Tapestry-Bees, although we may also find their nests in holes in wells; and we have ourselves dislodged them from an old and disused padlock. Two or three days give sufficient time for this industrious little insect to tunnel away the earth from its burrow, as well as to upholster it with its coloured and dainty vegetable

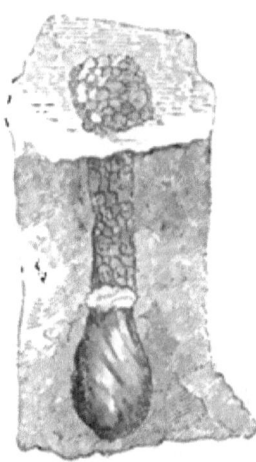

Finished Cell of TAPESTRY-BEE, *as seen in section.*

TAPESTRY-BEE.

hangings. The eggs are soon hatched, and the young grubs find sufficient stores of food for them in their subterranean retreat. Here they speedily grow strong enough to push the earth aside and appear above ground. This bee is little larger than the common House-fly, and is of a blackish colour, the belly being grey and silky; so that the young naturalist may readily identify it by the latter characters.

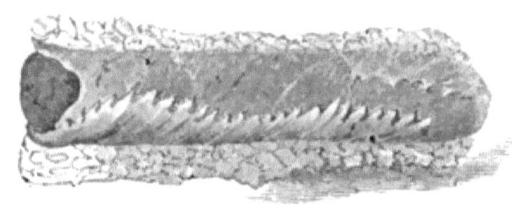

OUTER CASE OF NEST OF LEAF-CUTTER BEE.

There is a family of hymenopterous insects termed *fossorial* because of their digging or burrowing. The name given to this family is *Pompilidæ*. One genus (*Pompilius*) is most abundant on our sandy heaths, although it is common everywhere in this country. Its burrow is dug out more especially as a safe nursery for its young, and it would appear as if only one egg were deposited in each of such underground abodes. It is then stocked with spiders, stung by the mother-insect so as to paralyze them and prevent their decomposing before the egg hatches, as they would do if they had been killed. When the grub emerges, it falls to and demolishes this prepared feast, and by the time the last spider has been eaten, the larva is ready to pass into the pupal state in the safe security which the instinct of its mother prepared for it. *Astata* is the name given by entomologists to a large-eyed insect frequent in sandpits and about sand-hills, where it can easily tunnel a subterranean nursery, about five inches long, for its young. This is then stocked as a larder with various kinds of insects. *Mellinurus* is another fossorial or burrowing bee, which can be readily identified by its yellow feet and the three yellow bands on its abdomen. It is very abundant in England, and its devices to catch flies for the purpose of storing its pantry are very remarkable. Mr. F. Smith, of the British Museum, tells us that as many as four or five females will lie in wait upon a patch of cow-dung until some luckless fly settles on it. When this happens, a cunning and gradual approach is made. A sudden attempt would not succeed, for the fly is the more rapid of flight, and therefore a degree of artifice is required. This is arranged by the *Mellinurus* running past the victim slowly, and apparently in an unconcerned manner, until the poor fly is caught unawares. As soon as the first fly is caught, the *Mellinurus* deposits its egg, and then proceeds to catch the necessary number of insects to serve as food for the voracious grub which will soon emerge from it. In Mr. Smith's "Catalogue" there may be found an account of other and less abundant species of Hymenoptera which lead partially underground lives in burrows excavated by themselves.

In many respects the manner with which another well-known insect, the COMMON WASP (*Vespa vulgaris*) surveys the ground for the site of the colony it intends to found reminds us of the procedure of the Humble-Bee. Like the latter, some hybernating female awakes from her winter's sleep in the sunshine, and begins to search for the proper situation in a hedge-bank. She also is not too proud to avail herself of the previous labours of some rat or mouse, and will commence on their deserted runs if necessary, and excavate a dome-shaped chamber. The Wasp is the

WASPS' NEST.

world's original *paper-maker*, and what is more, adopts a method which human paper-manufacturers have only recently discovered—she uses wood-pulp. The latter is the material, light and strong, which the female founder of a "nest" employs to build up the wonderful structure she now proceeds to rear within the spacious hollow her own industry has dug out! To some root she has come across in her excavations, she attaches a short pillar made of this masticated pulp. At its lower portion there will be formed small cells, in which certain eggs are first laid, and each cell is then carefully covered with a roof made of the same material as the walls. Cells continue to be added one by one, and eggs deposited in them as they are made, so that the indefatigable industry of the foundress is marvellous. For, not only has the work of construction to go on thus rapidly, but the builder has to fetch and prepare her own materials. Before long another claim will be made on her anxiety —the first deposited eggs will have hatched into hungry grubs requiring to be constantly fed! There is only the original founder as yet to attend to all this work. But presently the earlier larvæ change into the pupal state, and after a rest, bite their way out of the cocoons they had formed over the mouth of their cells, and issue forth into the nest as perfect insects. These first-fledged wasps, as in the economy of the Humble-Bee, are *working* insects, capable of relieving her to whose labour they are indebted for life and shelter. Worker-insects are usually *undeveloped* females, and therefore cannot lay eggs; but by feeding them on special food the Hive-Bees can develop worker-grubs into fruitful or fully developed females. The latter are called "Queens," and such we find among the Wasps as well as Bees. The worker-wasps masticate the material for constructing fresh cells, and also excavate the earth around to make the original chamber capacious enough to receive them. Tier after tier of cells is thus elaborately constructed, each tier supported by strong taper pillars. The entire colony is also encased with numerous layers of specially masticated paper, which thus upholsters the earthen walls of the chamber, and prevents the soil from falling in. As with the Humble-Bees so here, at the close of the year all the members of this wonderful colony die off, except the few females so strangely selected to continue the race, and preserve it from extinction.

Another species of Wasp is very abundant, and may be distinguished from that just described by the three spots which occur on the first ring of the yellow abdomen. This species usually selects sound wood for masticating into the paper of its cell and walls, whilst the common Wasp prefers that which is decaying and therefore softer. The former is known to naturalists by the name of *Vespa germanica*. A third species, also devoted to burrowing habits, may be identified by a black anchor-like mark on the top of its head, as well as by its orange-coloured legs. This is the Red Wasp (*Vespa rufa*).

"Solitary" Wasps, as the members of this group are called which do not live in communities, are perhaps not so numerous in species as the Bees—in England, at least. The best-known of them is called *Odynerus muraria*—a species which excavates an underground dwelling, and, with the connected particles of sand or soil excavated, builds a vertical, tubular entrance to it as well. This tubular anteroom is always curved. When the subterranean chamber is finished, the wasp lays an egg at the further end, and then crams the burrow with little fat caterpillars she has carefully selected for the purpose. The anteroom is then taken down, and the mouth of the burrow filled up with earth; whilst within its darksome cavity the young grub feeds on its store of food, and passes through its necessary metamorphoses.

The soil beneath our feet is likewise a shelter and a retreat for the larvæ of many species of beetles, and even of some moths and dipterous flies. In some instances even the perfect insect resorts to subterranean habits. Perhaps the most lovely of all our British Coleoptera, although one of them of so fierce a nature that it has earned for itself the popular name of the Tiger-Beetle (*Cicindela campestris*), belongs to these occasional "Cave Dwellers." On sunny sand-banks we may find the vertical burrows of the Tiger-Beetles, excavated however by the larvæ to the depth of as much as a foot. There, with bulldog-like courage and tiger-like fierceness, we may see the head of the larva, armed with its fatal sickle-like jaws, lying flush with the mouth of its cave, waiting for some silly fly, or indeed any other entomological victim, to come within its deadly grasp. Its head is of enormous size compared with that of the perfect insect; and uncouth, shapeless grub though it look, out of all proportions of symmetry (for it seems to be hump-backed), it can ascend its vertical sand excavated tunnel with considerable alacrity, and maintain itself for hours at the mouth by means of peculiar hooks which proceed from the hump-like projection. These are used as sand-anchors, and are fixed firmly in the side of the hollow whilst the larva watches for its prey. Nothing can exceed the beauty, either of shape or colour, of the fully developed beetle, with its fine crimson-spotted, shining, emerald-green wing-cases and burnished belly. Unlike beetles in general, it is rapid of flight as well as fleet of foot,—habits which peculiarly fit it to be so successfully carnivorous. It is peculiarly fond of sunshine, and may be seen running about in the neighbourhood of the burrows of the larvæ. Possibly the idle but interested observer, who is reclining in such a place, may become aware of the presence of this insect by the fragrant perfume of sweet-briar which it emits. The adult beetle has not put off, in its final metamorphosis, the ferocity of its youth. Rather it has intensified it. Mr. Staveley tells us that the female has often been known to dismember and eat her husband! And Mr. Holmes relates that in captivity the Tiger-Beetles will fight most savagely, and actually rear themselves up against each other whilst combating like two bulldogs. One beetle will often decapitate its antagonist by a single stroke of its jaws.

We have five British species of *Cicindela*, the larvæ of most of which are underground dwellers; digging pits and lying in wait for their prey, and after capturing it sinking down to the bottoms of their dark abodes, there to devour it. These burrows are dug out by the jaws and front legs of the grub, and the sand is jerked backwards and out of the hole by its broad flat head. Sea-side visitors may find one species of this genus whose burrows are made in the soft blown sand-hills.

In competition with the quick run and rapid flight of the Tiger-Beetles is the swift, straight flight of the Dor-Beetles (*Geotrupes*). They are, perhaps, the most noticeable for our purpose. One of the many species of this genus is the "Shard-borne Beetle, with his drowsy hum," of Shakespere; how clumsy and powerless it is to direct its too rapid flight aright is proved by the uncomfortable way with which it will sometimes strike against people when out for an evening walk. Their bodies are of that beautiful metallic lustre which, in England at least, seems to be almost limited to the adornment of the Coleoptera. It is of a blue, steely tint, beautiful to behold. Unlike the Tiger-Beetles, the fully developed Dor performs the task of excavating the burrow. The hole is dug perpendicularly to the depth of six or eight inches. When completed, the diligent mother carries the dung of some animal to the bottom, and deposits an egg within pellets made of the ordure. This process is continued until all her eggs are laid. Sometimes the Dor-Beetles will commence their underground excavations under or near some cattle-droppings, for the sake of being near the substance in which their eggs are enveloped. When the latter hatch, the young grubs thus find themselves surrounded by what nature has selected as their food. In most of these subterranean toils, the work of excavation, as well as of preparation for the future progeny, falls upon the females. The scientific name of the Dor-Beetles (*Geotrupes*) is derived from the Greek, and signifies "earth-diggers." They also go by the name of "Dung-Beetles," from their habit of burying that material. That they do much good thereby, not only by clearing away ordure, but also by manuring and enriching the soil at some depth from the surface, is self-evident.

Scarcely less useful are the "Burying-Beetles" (*Necrophaga*), which bury the carcases of any dead animal or bird beneath the soil. This they do by excavating the soil from underneath the body, until a pit is made sufficiently deep for it to sink into below the level of the surface. In the carcase the eggs of the beetle are deposited, or rather those of several beetles,

BURYING-BEETLES AT WORK.

for the excavation has been a combined operation. It is then covered over, and the larvæ, when hatched, find themselves in the very midst of abundant food. It is astonishing to find how soon one of these Burying or Sexton Beetles, as they are also called, will scent out a dead and decaying body. What the keen nostril of the Vulture does for garbage of a more pronounced kind, that of the Sexton Beetle does for the numerous dead bodies of moles, mice, rats, birds, etc. That a very large number of the latter animals must die every year is very evident, yet how seldom we see their carcases lying about. This is because the Sexton Beetles clear them away and bury them out of sight almost as soon as they are dead. "Dust to dust" is the ultimate end of the bodies of animals as well as of men. How laborious is the self-imposed toil of these insects may be seen from the following incident. M. Gleiditsch watched *four* of these beetles, which buried the bodies of four frogs, three birds, two fishes, one mole, two grasshoppers, the entrails of a fish, and two pieces of meat in one small area of earth!

The larvæ of several species of beetles are only too well known to farmers and graziers by the name of "Wire-Worms." This name, however, is made to include the grubs of other insects than beetles, for those of the common Crane-Fly, or "Daddy Longlegs," also go by this name. The true Wire-Worms, however, are the larvæ of a family of beetles called *Elateridæ*, or "Leapers." In the adult state the insect is known by the popular name of "Skip-Jack," from the power of jerking itself up several inches in the air when it happens to fall on its back. When suddenly overtaken by supposed danger, it resorts to a very cunning stratagem, employed by various kinds of insects, and shams death. Its eggs are laid in the ground, and there hatch into long, narrow, eyeless grubs, called, on account of the toughness of their skins, "Wire-Worms." Even when trodden upon and rolled over by a grass roller, they are uninjured, and are, perhaps, only pressed deeper into the soil. These worms feed on potato and other roots of vegetables, and are especially abundant on lawns and in grass meadows, where they injure the herbage by destroying the white thread-like roots which so greatly resemble their own bodies. Indeed few roots are free from their attacks. Here comes in the usefulness of many of our wild birds, and of some of our underground mammalia. The Mole is a keen and ruthless destroyer of the Wire-Worm, hunting for it even in preference to the common earth-worm. The Rook, Starling, and other birds pick them out and devour them by countless millions. No other larva of beetle takes so long a time to pass into the adult stages as this notorious grub. A single summer with other species is usually sufficient. Not so with the Wire-Worm. As if well aware that its larval life is surrounded by abundance and variety of food, it does not hurry to pass on to an advanced stage of development; and hence it remains a Wire-Worm for as long as four or five summers in succession, so that one individual thus devours as much as four or five grubs of other species of beetles, of different habits, would do.

The larvæ of the common Cockchafer (*Melolontha vulgaris*) are sometimes erroneously called "Wire-Worms." That matters little, however, for they have, in many respects, similar habits. The female beetle lays her eggs in the soil, and these, when hatched, commence immediately to feed on any succulent roots in their neighbourhood. At first they are small, and then are mistaken for Wire-Worms, but ere long they grow large and fat almost to bursting. So voracious are they in their feeding, as we are told by the Rev. J. G. Wood, that sometimes they so completely destroy the grass that the turf will become detached, and may be rolled up by the hand as easily as if the turf-cutter's spade had passed under it. Not only grass roots, but those of any other vegetable, are attacked and devoured by these voracious Cockchafer grubs, potatoes being especially held in favour by them as an article of diet. Were it not for those beneficial friends of the farmer, the Rooks, the damage done to vegetable crops of all kinds by these larvæ would be enormous.

In September we may see the dewy grass of our meadows swarming with "Daddy Longlegs" (*Tipula longicornis*). They are only females, however, which we see so abundantly, and they are engaged in the work of piercing the ground to receive their eggs. Only one egg is laid in each hole, so that a good deal of labour has to be expended before it is finished. The young are hatched in the ground, and begin to feed on the tender roots of the grass. They soon become as tough-skinned grubs as the true wire-worms for which they are often mistaken. The thousands of Daddy Longlegs to be seen in every field engaged in the work of ovipositing, plainly shows us what an innumerable host of larvæ would destroy our grass if they were not kept down. The Starling is unquestionably the bitterest foe of these underground pests, and destroys thousands of them. Therefore we ought to encourage these pretty birds

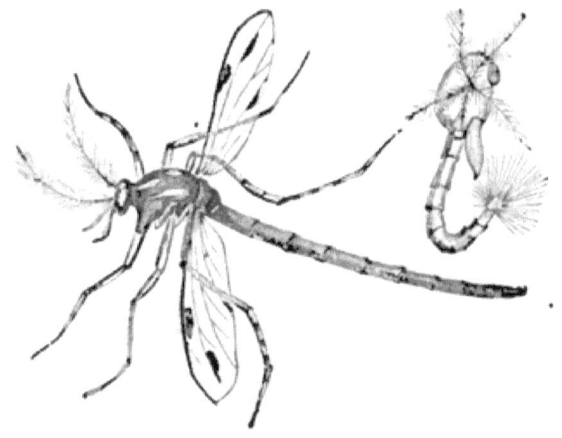

CRANE-FLY (*Tipula longicornis*).

when they appear on our lawns, or crowd our fields in flocks, for they are then engaged in the friendly and useful occupation of destroying foes which all our own ingenuity does not enable us to get at. The ungainly legs of the Crane-Fly, or "Daddy-long-legs," are only seen to advantage when we watch the female stalking about in the grass, and looking for a place wherein to lay her eggs.

The pupæ of some species of moths are fain to creep for shelter to the bosom of mother Earth, and to find underground a protection from their numerous enemies. The largest of our British moths is the "Death's Head" (*Acherontia atropos*), and its huge, full-fed larvæ burrow into the soil, and there undergo their final transformations. The pupæ of numerous other species have to be "dug" out of the earth by the collector, attached underground to the bark or roots of trees. The same subterranean abode furnishes a retreat for earwigs, centipedes, and a host of other creatures which come under the popular denomination of "crawling."

CHAPTER IV.

UNDERGROUND SOCIETIES.

We have waited, however, for a special opportunity of speaking more fully of perhaps the most interesting animals in the world, from whatever point of view we study them, small though they are. Long before human civilization had begun to spread, or the latest doctrine of political economy had been taught (that of "division of labour"), there had been existing underground communities both *monarchical*, as in the case of the bees and wasps, and partly *republican*, as with the ants. The naturalist takes no heed of the distinctions which have so much influence with the ignorant—those of mere bigness and littleness. The habits of ants, therefore, have always been the most interesting among entomological pursuits—" Our six-legged competitors," Sir John Lubbock, their modern historian, designates them; and certainly it is wonderful into how small a body so much sense and wisdom can be condensed! If men were as wise, in proportion to their greater size and bulk, as the Ants, the highest flights of modern science would appear but as the fairy-tales which amuse our children.

Perhaps not even Huber has more carefully studied the habits of insects than Sir John Lubbock, and his papers contributed to and published in the Transactions of the Linnean Society of London are marvels of amusing, patient research and observation. At the recent meeting of the British Association (1878), in an address on this subject, Sir John stated that he had kept about thirty species of ants in confinement. They throve well there, and he had some then living which he had kept four years, and these were probably bred the year before, so that they were then five years old. It is well known, and was first remarked by Huber, that one species of ant collects the eggs of plant-lice (*Aphides*) and takes them to its nests. There the ants watch them with the greatest care until they are hatched. The ants are very fond of sweets, and plant-lice have the power of secreting a sweet juice sometimes found on the surface of leaves, and called "honey-dew." This the ants lap up with amazing greed, and will wander on and about the shrubs which are supporting such desirable animals. In short, the ants regard these *aphides* as we do cows, and can actually excite them to secrete the much-desired nectar by stroking them with their antennæ. Some species of ants are content with obtaining their nectar in this fashion; but those to which we have referred actually carry off the eggs, hatch them, and keep the *aphides* in confinement, as we keep cattle, for the sake of the liquid sweetness they can be induced to emit! The ants will even tend these plant-lice in their underground retreats throughout the whole winter, although they cannot be of the slightest service to them during that period.

The sense of smell possessed by ants is remarkably delicate, although it differs in intensity in various species. No observations, however, have as yet indicated that they possess any sense of *hearing*. They are capable of distinguishing colours, and appear to be very sensitive to that of violet. Sir John Lubbock has proved not only that the ants of one nest or republic know each other, but that they actually remembered each other after a year's separa-

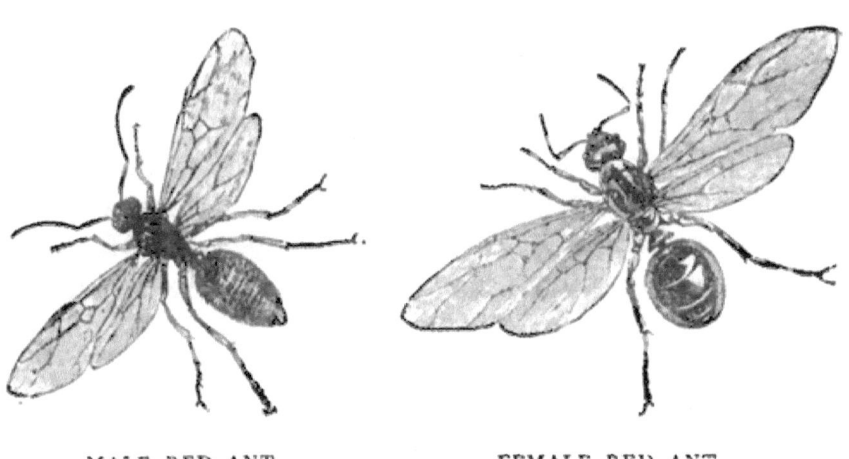

MALE RED ANT (*Formica rufa*).   FEMALE RED ANT (*Formica rufa*).

tion! This he has proved by experiment, and has shown the various signs of gladness exhibited on their meeting after these long lapses of time.

As Mr. Staveley has remarked, "it is possible to believe almost anything of the Ants!" Not only are they the most skilful of architects in the construction of their underground cities, but as statesmen, landed proprietors, herdsmen, slave-owners, and even agriculturists, they stand prominently at the head of the insect world. No other class of insects is so amenable to the self-appointed laws of its communities. We have already referred to ants which

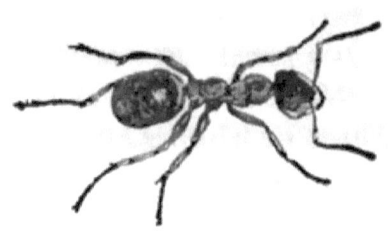

WORKER OF RED ANT (*Formica rufa*).

are *herdsmen,* in that they rear, keep, and tend *aphides* as we do milch kine. We have now to refer to several species which actually go forth on marauding expeditions, and bring home the defeated members of another species whose colony has been surprised, as *slaves!* One of the most notable of these slave-making species is the Blood-red Ant (*Formica sanguinea*), so called from the blood-red colour of the females. No fewer than four different species of ant are liable to be attacked and brought home as slaves by this kind. Such an unlooked-for habit is worthy of a brief notice, and nobody has described it better than the late Mr. Edward Newman. He says, " The time for capturing slaves extends over a period of about ten weeks, and never commences until the males and females are about emerging from the pupa state, and then the ruthless marauders never interfere with the continuance of a species. This instinct seems specially provided, for were the Slave Ants created for no other end than to fill the station of slavery to which they appear to be doomed, still even that service must fail were the attacks to be made on their nests before the winged multitudes have departed, or are departing, charged with the duty of continuing their kind.

"When the Red Ants are about to sally forth on a marauding expedition, they send scouts to ascertain the exact position in which a colony of negroes are to be found. These scouts, having discovered the object of their search, return to the nest and report their success. Shortly afterwards the army of Red Ants marches forth, headed by a vanguard, which is perpetually changing; the individuals which constitute it, when they have advanced a little beyond the main body, halting, falling into the rear, and being replaced by others. This vanguard consists of eight or ten ants only. When they have arrived near the negro colony, they disperse, wandering through the herbage, and hunting about as if aware of the propinquity of the object of their search, yet ignorant of its exact position. At last they discover the settlement, and the foremost of the invaders, rushing impetuously to the attack, are met, grappled with, and frequently killed by the negroes on guard. The alarm is quickly communicated to the interior of the nest; the negroes sally forth by thousands, and, the Red Ants rushing to the rescue, a desperate conflict ensues, which, however, always terminates in the defeat of the negroes, who retire to the inmost recesses of their habitations. Now follows the scene of pillage. The Red Ants, with their powerful mandibles, tear open the sides of the negro ant-hill, and rush into the heart of the

THE ANTS' BATTLE-FIELD.

citadel. In a few minutes each of the invaders emerges, carrying in its mouth the pupa of a working negro, which it has obtained in spite of the vigilance and valour of its natural guardians. The Red Ants return in perfect order to their nest, bearing with them their living burdens. On reaching the nest, the pupæ appear to be treated precisely as their own, and the workers, when they emerge, perform the various duties of the community with the greatest energy and apparent goodwill. They prepare the nest, take the pupæ into the sunshine, and perform every office which the welfare of the community seems to require. In fact, they conduct themselves as if fulfilling their original destination!"

Sir John Lubbock tells us that in one species of ant this habit of kidnapping has begotten such an entire dependence of the captors on their slaves that they would perish even in the midst of plenty if left to themselves! The vile practice seems to have brought with it its own punishment. Sir John Lubbock records how he kept some of these ants alive for months by giving them a slave for one hour every day to clean and feed them! The same careful observer expresses it as his opinion that the various communities of ants offer numerous analogies to those of men. He thinks the slave-making ants represent an abnormal, and perhaps only a temporary state of things, and that the slave-making species will eventually find it impossible to compete with those which are more self-dependent and have reached a higher phase of ant-civilization.

Sir John Lubbock has also ingeniously drawn a comparison between the various conditions of life exemplified by different species of ants, and the earlier stages in the development of human civilization. Thus we have hunting, pastoral, and even agricultural ants. Some species, such as *Formica fusca*, live principally on the produce of the chase, for, though they feed partly on the honey-dew of *aphides*, they have not domesticated these insects. Such species probably retain the habits once common to all kinds of ants; and it is evident they offer a parallel to the lower races of mankind, who live mainly by hunting. Like the latter, this species of ant live in comparatively small communities, and the instincts of collective action are little developed among them. They hunt singly, and their battles are single combats, like those of early history. Such other species of ants as *Lasius flavus*, however, represent a distinctly higher type of social life. They may literally be said to have domesticated certain species of *aphides*, and can be compared to the pastoral stage of human progress—to the races which live on the produce of their flocks and herds. Their communities are more numerous, they act more in concert, their battles are no longer mere duels or single combats, for they know how to act in combination. Sir John Lubbock hazards the conjecture that the latter species will gradually exterminate the mere hunting species, just as savages disappear before more advanced races. Lastly, the agricultural nations may be compared with the Harvesting Ants (which are not British species, however). The life-history of the Agricultural Ants of Texas—a species which actually *cultivates* a particular kind of grass around its dwellings, and weeds away all others that would interfere with its growth—is the crowning point of our account of these "six-legged competitors" of ours.

Let us now direct our attention to the mode of constructing their underground cities. From the loose appearance of an ant-hill we should little imagine there extended beneath a well and architecturally arranged dwelling-place, capable of sheltering the different kinds of these insects. We see only an apparently loose heap, with hosts of ants appearing to glide purposelessly about it. Each colony consists of males, females, and workers, although the entire labour falls on the latter. Not even among the bees and wasps have we an illustration of greater industry than is exhibited by these much smaller insects. The Brown Ants (*Formica brunnea*) form their nest or colony in a series of stories, each about the third of an inch in height. The partitions are exceedingly thin, but they are so well finished that the inner walls present a smooth and unbroken surface. These storied chambers lie upon one another to the ground floor. The latter communicates with subterranean chambers and passages.

Like other species, the common Brown Ants do not follow an invariable plan in the construction of their nests, but modify them according to circumstances. As a rule, however, they are formed of concentric suites of chambers. In each suite there are a number of these chambers or halls, lodges of narrow dimensions, and long galleries for general accommodation. The arched ceilings, covering the most spacious places, are supported either by little columns, slender walls, or regular buttresses. There are also chambers which have but one entrance, which communicate with the lower story, as well as large open spaces which serve as a kind of cross-roads, and into these all the streets or passages of the underground city terminate. An ant-hill often contains more than twenty stories in that upper portion which usually rises above the ground, and quite as many beneath the surface. It is owing to this construction of the nest that the ants can regulate the heat so as to suit their purpose. When the sun is too hot and overheats the upper floors or stories, they withdraw the pupæ stored in the nurseries there to the cooler and moister chambers below ground; and when these lower suites of rooms become uninhabitable during a rainy season, the ants then transfer their charge to the higher stories.

M. Huber has related his personal observation of the construction of an ant's nest. He noticed that as the nest proceeded in its development the ants kept within during the day, or only went forth by subterranean galleries, which opened some feet away from the nest. There were two or three openings at the surface of the latter, but none of the workers were seen to pass out that way, on account of its being so much exposed to the sun. The ants' nest then gradually rose in the midst of the grass to a roundish form. The ants worked most in the early morning, when the dew was not as yet evaporated. They then began to make fresh apertures; by-and-by a gentle rain fell, and the ants began to build in earnest, and soon, says M. Huber, all their architectural talents were brought into full play. When the rain commenced, great numbers of ants quitted their underground abode, re-entered it almost immediately, and then returned, bearing between their jaws little pellets of earth, which they deposited on the roof of their nest. These pellets were the foundations of little walls, which soon started upon all sides, having spaces left between them. In several places columns were ranged at regular distances, and in this way the rough beginning of a new story was commenced. Each ant formed the pellet of earth by scraping with its mandibles the bottom of its abode. A little mass of earth was then kneaded and moulded at will, and could be easily applied to the spot where it had to remain. There it was pressed so as to fill up any inequalities of the surface of the wall. Whilst thus engaged, the ants work their antennæ, or *feelers*, over and about every particle of earth as soon as the latter is placed in its proper position, and the whole was then pressed down by their fore-feet. After having traced out the place of their masonry, in laying here and there foundations for the pillars and partitions they were about to erect, the insects gradually raised them higher by the addition of fresh materials. In constructing a gallery, two little walls would be raised opposite to each other, and when at the height of nearly half an inch the space between them would be covered in with vaulted ceiling.

Having made the partitions of a sufficient height, the ants quitted their labours in the upper part of the building, and then affixed to the upper and interior part of each wall fragments of moistened earth in an almost horizontal direction, and in such a way as to form a ledge, which, by being extended, could be made to join a similar ledge coming from the opposite wall. On one side several vertical partitions were seen to form the scaffolding of a ledge, which communicated with several corridors by apertures formed in the masonry. On another side a regular formed hall was erected, the vaulted ceiling of which was sustained by numerous pillars. Further off might be recognized the rudiments of one of the cross-roads already mentioned. These parts of the ants' nest were the most spacious, but the ants never appeared embarrassed in constructing the ceilings as to how to cover them in, although they were often more than two inches in breadth ! They laid the foundations of this ceiling in the upper part of the angles formed by the different walls, and from the tops of the pillars, as from so many centres, layers of earth, horizontal and slightly convex, were carried forward to meet the several portions coming from different points of what M. Huber called the large public thoroughfare. It might be thought that these ceilings, supported only by a few pillars, must decrepitate and fall to ruin under the rain which continually dropped upon them. Not so, however, for the earth adhered on the slightest contact, and the rain, instead of loosening the particles, seemed to bind them together. Indeed rain is actually necessary to these underground workers, both to cement their work together, and to smooth down its inequalities. Of course, we are here speaking of an ordinary shower, for very violent rains often do the nests much harm. So hard do the ants toil that M. Huber says it took them only seven or eight hours to construct one tier or story, and that the moment they had finished this they untiringly began upon another! As with human builders, mistakes are frequently made during the progress of these subterranean excavations, and then we find the mistake is corrected, for a piece of work will be taken down, and put up again in the right fashion.

A writer in *Science-Gossip* for 1870, who had for some time kept ants in what he calls a "Formicary," gives the following very interesting account of the way of life underground of the Black Ants:—"The curiosity they exhibit about any fresh object is great. One day when they were very quiet, and few above ground, I took the opportunity to re-paper the platform, to pump the water from the trough, and to clean it out. Though it was dry about half an hour, only one ant came down to it, yet when all was completed, and the moat refilled, in about ten minutes there was a constant stream of ants descending to look at the alterations, which they had so rapidly detected. Whenever one ant meets another, they cross antennæ,

GLASS FORMICARY FOR OBSERVING THE HABITS OF ANTS.

and pass on, and I have never seen two ants actually meet without giving this salutation.

"Ants are of three kinds,—males or drones, females, and workers. The first two appear to have only to do with the production of eggs, and apparently take no share in the nursing. The males are hardly so big as an ordinary neuter, but are of a darker colour, and possess large and spreading wings. The females are nearly as large as an ordinary wasp, and have very lengthy wings indeed. When I stocked my formicary I put in neither males nor females, trusting to some of both kinds appearing in the cocoons, and as several of these were half as large again as others, I do not doubt that it was from them that some of my females were hatched. My first female appeared on the 2nd of August, and my first male on the 13th, and in the end I had over a dozen of the former, and still more of the latter. In fine weather the males and females might often be seen poking their heads out of the openings by the grass, and occasionally walking a few steps out, but they always appeared dazed at the sight of the outer world; and it was evidently the object of the workers to prevent them from straying, for I have many times seen them, when a female has thus emerged, give her a push in front, or a kind of bite behind, upon which she would turn round and quietly disappear. They once even dragged bodily below one of the males which had wandered away, and who would not obey their usual signals. The males and females might often be seen lying in a burrow, perfectly motionless, and enjoying the warmth, whilst the neuters were hard at work all around them. Once when I touched with my spatula the antennæ of a female which was looking out, it was wonderful to see the rage with which one of the neuters wished to attack the assailant!

"The great instinct of an ant, and that which overcomes all others, is care for its cocoons. Turn over an ant-hill, and the first thing you see are excited ants running in all directions carrying them into shelter. Once I added about thirty cocoons from another nest. It was wonderful to see the eaters of any introduced morsel forsake their meat, the workers leave their burrows, and the stragglers their amusement, and one and all setting to work with a will. In ten minutes not a cocoon was left above ground. That they take them down deeper in the nest in the evening, or in cold weather, I have repeated instances of. I have often turned over an ant-hill at both of these seasons, and not a cocoon was to be seen. I have gone deep, however, and have found numbers; but when I have opened an ant-hill on a warm day, I have always seen them in clusters close to the surface. Heat is evidently necessary for the due hatching of ants' cocoons. It was on the 20th of July that they first brought out a few cocoons, and laid them in the passages against the glass of my formicary. When the time for removal came, this office was told off to a single ant, although many others were swarming in all the passages. The ant carried the cocoons about half the length of the formicary, and depositing them just inside a hole, went for its next load. I always knew him by the unusual pace at which he hurried along. From this time until they were all hatched, the cocoons appeared whenever the sun shone upon the formicary, numbers of ants helping in the operation. Some were kept out an hour or more; and others only five or ten minutes.

"Once when it was a very cloudy day, I took a candle and fastened it close to that portion of the glass at which the ants generally put their cocoons. They felt the heat directly, and in ten minutes more cocoons were out than I ever saw before. Males, females, and neuters were abundant; and, at one time, the passages behind the candle were quite black with the clusters of ants swarming to the warmth. On the 8th of September, when the colony was very lively from the warmth of a candle, I had the good fortune to see a young ant actually leave its cocoon. When I first saw it it was half out of the case, and had there stuck. One neuter had fast hold of it, whilst another pulled at the remainder of its covering. But it was a difficult matter, and it was a long time before they got by degrees the young one out. A kind of stringy piece, however, still remained joined to one end of the cocoon, and entangled in the legs of the embryo. After much trouble this was cut through, and the young ant was at last safely and completely freed."

The males and females of all our species of Social Ants leave the nest when they have arrived at perfection, and associate together in large numbers in the atmosphere for a short time. After this the males die, and only the females return to the nest. There they cut off, or have cut off for them, their gauzy but no longer required wings, and set to work, to labour diligently until there is a sufficient number of the "workers" hatched to relieve them of their toil. In this respect there is a great similarity between the bees, wasps, and ants. After the workers have appeared on the scene, the principal business of the females is to lay eggs. Dr. Staveley says of these eggs that "they are tended with the greatest care by

ANTS PREPARING FOR FLIGHT.

the workers, who carry them from the place where they are dropped, and carefully deposit them in suitable chambers, moistening them, it is said, from their own mouths, and thus probably affording that nourishment which must be essential to their *growth*, the eggs of ants growing larger after they are laid. According to the observations of M. Huber, the nurses then bestow the most assiduous attention upon the eggs, daily removing them to those parts of the nest where the temperature is most suitable. The eggs hatched, still further labours devolve upon the careful and busy nurses, who to the daily removal of their little charges (creatures which before long are equal to themselves in size) now add the task of supplying them with food; or rather, of feeding them. Nor does their care end here. When the time for its perfection arrives, the larva, having spun its own cocoon (the only act which it is ever allowed to do for itself), is not only extricated by the workers from its silken shroud, but even receives their assistance in divesting itself of the delicate membrane which still has to be stripped from its body!" Well might the wise man advise the sluggard to "Go to the ant; consider her ways and be wise;" for in comparison with its size its indefatigable industry is unequalled in the entire animal world. Moreover, one is obliged not only to assent to the "division of labour" which it has been the highest glory of political economy to have discovered, but to the existence among these social communities of a principle more lofty and sacred still—that of self-denial and devotion to the welfare of others. These little sexless insects, incapable of bringing forth young on which their own care and affection may be bestowed, nevertheless devote themselves to the welfare of the community to which they belong, and labour for its goodwill and perpetuity with an ardour and zeal and devotion which equal the loftiest efforts of human patriotism!

During the winter the remaining ants lie torpid in the lower stories of their nests. We say "remaining," for immense numbers both of the males and females, when they resort to the winged state in August, are consumed by birds, or blown in masses into the sea. Were it not so, the marvellous fecundity of the tribe is such that we should be completely overrun by them.

The Wood Ant, or Pismire (*Formica rufa*) is the largest of our native species. From its size it is frequently called the "Horse" Ant, and from its large nests, the "Hill" Ant. Every one who has wandered in fir-woods must have noticed the large hillocks which these insects contrive to raise. In order to form this enormous nest, Mr. Wood tells us, the ants travel to great distances, always following some definite track which in course of time will be plainly evident to the eye. When once these ants have taken to a track, they adhere to it, and many successive generations continue to use it. Mr. Wood further states that he has been shown ant-roads by old men who said they had themselves been familiar with them from their earliest recollection! The outside of the nest of the Wood Ant is composed of whatever materials the insects can most easily find, although the needle-shaped leaves of the pine-trees and sticks appear to be most common. Pieces of wood, small pebbles, shells, grains of wheat, oats, or barley, &c., may also be found on these often huge heaps, which rise in a conical fashion so that the rain can easily run off them. The Wood Ants do not construct long covered or underground ways, as it appears they have fewer enemies to guard against than the Yellow or Brown Ants. The nest of the Wood Ants is at first simply a hollow in the earth, excavated in part by themselves, although they do not object to take advantage of any favourable site prepared for them. Some of the insects taking possession may then be seen roaming about in search of materials for the outside work, whilst others are employed in mixing the earth which has been dug out with fragments of wood, leaves, &c. Another company of ants are acting as labourers to the latter, and are constantly bringing them materials. In this

THE ANT-HILL.

way the edifice increases in size and complexity daily. Here and there small openings are left, which will be made into galleries leading to the exterior by-and-by. The roof now becomes convex, to keep off the rain, which rarely penetrates to more than half an inch in depth. The under portion of the nest is excavated into spacious halls, for the purpose of receiving the larvæ. These halls communicate with various galleries. Even the rain assists in the work, and helps to bind the entire colony into a strong edifice. During the day, the Wood Ants go out foraging, bringing home flies, caterpillars, or grubs of any sort. At night, before going to their short rest, every door or opening leading to the nest is carefully closed, and at no small expenditure of labour. Similarly during wet days these ants rarely go out, or take down their shutters, or unbar their doors !

Speaking of the industry of these wonderful insects, the Rev. J. G. Wood very aptly says :—" Compare the size of an ant with that of a man, and then see how vast are the powers of so small a creature. Taking all the calculations in round numbers, and very much to the disadvantage of the Ant, we find that a single man, who would have achieved a similar work in a single day, must have acted as follows :—

"He must have excavated two parallel trenches, each of seventy-two feet in length and four feet six inches in depth ; he must have made bricks from the clay he dug out, and with them built a wall along each side the trenches, from two to three feet in height and fourteen or fifteen inches in thickness ; and lastly, he must have gone over the whole of his work again, and smoothed the interior until it was exactly true, straight, and level. All this work must also have been done without the least assistance, and the ground must be supposed to be filled with huge boulders, and covered with tree-trunks, broken logs, and other impediments !"

Various kinds of beetles, and one peculiar kind,

known to entomologists as *Quedius brevis*, is frequently found living in the burrows and galleries of the Wood Ant, as a kind of "messmates." These insects appear to have adopted these underground shelters for protection's sake, and the ants kindly tolerate them, although they could so readily destroy them, and are so strongly carnivorous in their diet, notwithstanding their fondness for sweets. Sir John Lubbock has shown that the habit of some of our wild flowers to close early in the day, may be as a defence against the depredations of the ants, when the evaporation of the dews enables them to roam over the vegetation. The presence of woolly hairs on flower-stems and leaves he also thinks may act as a *chevaux-de-frise* against the climbing of ants, which would otherwise suck the nectar of the flowers without being able to cross them by carrying away pollen, as winged insects do.

Just as there are solitary wasps and bees as distinguished from the social communities, where the highest degree of insect civilization is to be seen, so there are a few species of solitary ants. The latter belong to the family *Mutillidæ*. As might be expected from the non-requirement of "division of labour" so necessary to communities, these solitary ants are not distinguished by possessing workers or neuters. The females are wingless, but the males winged. The former have legs specially adapted for excavating the sand where they live, and for defence have a powerful sting. We may see them about sand-banks, where the female of one species, *M. Europæa*, is a stout, smooth-bodied, wingless, red and black ant, about two-thirds of an inch long. The winged male is of much smaller size. The larvæ are hatched and brought up underground, so that they are among the numerous creatures which, even in our own country, Mother Earth takes into her capacious bosom for shelter and protection!

CHAPTER V.

EARTH-WORMS.

But perhaps of all the myriad animal forms which at some period or another of their lives inhabit the soil beneath us, none can be regarded as so entirely and thoroughly adapted to an underground existence as those creatures which, for this very reason, we term the "Earth-worms." How familiar we are all with its appearance, although few of us are so acutely intimate with its general habits and life-history. For ages it has been regarded as the very type of a degraded, humiliated being—its life a curse, its whole existence at once a punishment and a warning! But we have now learned better. We have seen that the soils of the earth, like the waters of the earth, have their special and more or less adapted sets of inhabitants which not only find in their adaptations the happiness of an existence, but at the same time testify to the Wisdom and Goodness which has placed them where we find them! In spite of its subterranean, crawling habits, the earth-worm is as perfect and happy, because as admirably fitted to the surroundings of the life it leads, as the joyous skylark or the frolicsome squirrel. It needs no apology from any one—rather, the life-history of the Earth-worm teaches a lesson to those who ignorantly pity or despise it.

The ringed body of the common Lob or Earth-worm (*Lumbricus terrestris*) has rows of bristles on the underside. The possession of these has given the name to the order of which it is a member, *Oligochæta*. These rows of bristles take the place of the foot-tubercles to be seen in the higher members of the *Annelida*, and, like the latter, they are organs of locomotion. Therefore, although the Earth-worm has no feet in the ordinary acceptation of the term, it has other special organs of locomotion which serve it quite as admirably as legs would. On account of these locomotive bristles of the Earth-worm being few in number, the name of the order, which signifies " few bristles," has been given. Altogether the worm has *eight* rows of these bristles. The mouth of this animal has no teeth, and it opens into a gullet which leads to a muscular crop, which latter is succeeded by a second dilatation or gizzard. Hence a complete physiological arrangement is made for whatever food passes through the body to have its entire nutriment absorbed from it. The intestine is continued straight to the anus, although it is somewhat hindered in its free course by the numerous transverse partitions which partly cross it. The blood circulation (or rather that which answers to it) is called *pseudo-hæmal*. It is aërated from outside the Earth-worm's body by means of a series of pouches, where it is exposed. These pouches allow the air to pass into the body by means of pores, which may be seen on the outside of each ring or segment of the worm's body. The locomotive bristles of which we have spoken are arranged in rows not only underneath each segment but along the sides as well. A full-grown earth-worm has about one hundred and twenty of such rings or segments. The body is highly elastic, as well as extremely muscular. Hence it can extend itself, or contract itself, in the most wonderful manner.

Of course, all this detail of structure can only be verified by much closer observation than popular notice takes of the creature. To people generally the Earth-worm appears as an object possessing neither head nor tail. It is regarded as a harmless, wriggling, slimy, and disagreeable thing; and is even supposed to prey upon the carcases of animals and men when placed in the ground. It is quite impossible the Earth-worm should devour anything of the sort. One of the best accounts of this very common, and in spite of popular prejudice, most *useful* creature, has appeared in *Science-Gossip* for 1878, from the pen of Professor Paley. He there speaks of the false estimate which people have ignorantly formed of the Earth-worm, and says: "The lob-worm may almost be called a clever and intelligent creature; very sly indeed of letting its mode of action be seen, but showing by certain results, which readily come under our observation, that it has instincts which fall very little short of reasoning and design!" And all this can be said of a lowly organized animal which, as Huxley says, has "no eyes, nor any other organs of special sense that are known!"

Professor Paley's remarks on the Earth-worm were supplemented and enlarged by the observations of

Mr. W. Budden, who has also devoted much time to the study of its habits. Both agree in ascribing to this hitherto much-despised creature instincts of anything but a low order. There are many difficulties in the way of ascertaining its habits, on account of its timidity and watchfulness; and also because it seldom habitually appears above the surface of the ground except at night. Again, as we have already said, it is one of the most permanent underground dwellers, and so passes the greater part of its life where we cannot see it. If we thrust a spade into the soil where worms abound, we may see several of them crawling out of the ground even at the distance of a yard or more, having been alarmed by the motion suddenly communicated to the earth in which they burrow. Then the Earth-worm may be seen stretched out to more than twice its ordinary length, whilst it grasps the earth with its bristle-armed joints, as with anchors, and so frees the fore part of its body to allow it to extend itself. As soon as this has been done, the segments or joints of this fore part anchor themselves by their bristles to the earth in their turn. The hinder part of the body is now set free, to contract and pull itself up to the advancing part. In this way locomotion takes place, after the simplest but still very admirably contrived fashion.

Although the Earth-worm has no eyes, people speak of their "seeing you." This is because of the remarkable power they have of detecting a footstep by the tremor communicated to the earth. Hence, if you are walking out some summer's evening, and see a worm extending half out of its hole, if you continue to advance you will notice that it withdraws itself within its burrow quite suddenly. Birds are well aware of the delicate sense of *touch* possessed by earth-worms, as we may see by the light manner in which blackbirds and thrushes will hop to worm-holes, so as to extract the dainty morsel before it is aware of its foes.

We take advantage of Professor Paley's most admirable observations to reproduce some of the best of them. He says :—

"The Lob-worm has a singular habit of filling up the entrance of its hole with fallen leaves, bits of stick or straw, feathers, or any small and light objects —it is rather fond of bits of string—that it finds near. If it cannot get these, it piles up a little hillock of pebbles, or small bits of lime, cinder, &c. Why it does this, it is not easy to make out. Possibly it is to allow the passage of air into the hole, and yet to prevent the intrusion of insects, such as beetles or ants, which would give it as much trouble and annoyance as a ferret gives to a rabbit in its burrow. For if it were solely for purposes of food, which fallen leaves or seeds of trees might be, and apparently are, the worm would not draw in such indigestible delicacies as string or feathers. Perhaps they pull in anything that they find soft and yielding, and make trial of its edible qualities at their leisure. Whatever be the reason, the holes are carefully stopped up in the way I have described. This seems, indeed, rather stupid ; because a knowing bird may regard the tufts upon worm-holes as so many points for attack ; but this is the habit of the creature, and as I once, and once only, caught a lob-worm actually at work, I shall describe what I saw, which I thought extremely curious.

"My attention was directed to the fact that if the small heaps of pebbles were cleared away from a worm-hole, they were sure to be replaced next morning. Suspecting they worked only at night, I went late one summer evening, after a shower of rain, to a bed in the garden which was very full of earthworms. Walking up to it on tip-toe, and with extreme care (for I was well aware that if it felt the footstep two or three yards off, it would retire into the hole), I was lucky enough to see one very big worm with its body about half out of the hole. I then stood for some time perfectly still, and watched it as it reached out its elastic head to a small pebble, and by a clever jerk, or possibly by its slimy moisture adhering to it, it drew the pebble to its hole and left it close to the edge. Thus it took another and another, and now I was able to explain what I had often noticed, that every pebble within a circle of about six inches was moved away and piled up over the hole. The worm took the circle, elongating its body, and moving east or west and to every point of the compass, so to say, till not a pebble was left within its reach. This I *saw*, and the reader may believe that it is a strictly accurate account, though it may seem to credit the creature with more intelligence then it has any right to possess."

Prof. Paley expresses it as his opinion that any one might see the Earth-worm perform this feat, any summer night, by the light of a lantern or candle. Mr. W. Budden, writing in the same magazine as that in which the above article appears, confirms and adds to the writer's experience. Mr. Budden's observations were carried on during the wet evenings of June 1878, generally in the dusk, his object being to discover by what means earth-worms dragged string, leaves, twigs, &c., along the ground to their holes. He says:—

"Very carefully and quietly placing a candle on the earth where a number of large worms were foraging round their holes, I took care to place decayed leaves, &c., within the radius of the circle swept by their operations. The objects placed within their reach being, however, too much the colour of the soil accurately and distinctly to be sure of the *modus operandi*, the thought suddenly occurred to me to try white paper. Tearing up little strips about three inches long, I gave them a single fold, and placed one within the reach of a foraging worm. Very soon its elongated head came in contact with the paper, and instead of twining its head round the paper I saw it put its head underneath. Carefully watching, I saw a lip on each side of the paper, which, being compressed between the two, the paper was held firmly as in a vice, and so dragged to its hole. Continuing the experiments with my paper bait, I saw distinctly that the worm can compress and almost flatten its head as easily as it can elongate it. When the head is rendered obtuse, it can extend it on each side of the mouth so as to form two large distinct lips, between which it took hold of the papers and dragged them to the hole; but this is only method No. 2. There is yet another, which at first I could scarcely understand. Observing a worm place its head under the white paper, so that its operation was invisible, I saw the paper, without any apparent means of motion, slowly, ghost-like moving along the dark ground to the hole of the worm. Its head was not *round* it, nor did its lips *enclose* any part of the paper, and yet it moved. Quietly and carefully, by candle-light, continuing for hours my observations, I saw that when it suited the creature's purpose best, it had yet a third method of attaching itself to its baits. The worm having retracted its head in the same way as when forming its lips, firmly *pressed* it for a moment *on to* the paper, and then apparently forming a sucker of its mouth, the paper was firmly attached to it, and so, without being held, except as the leathern toy attaches itself by exhaustion of air to the stone, the paper followed the retreating worm and was dragged to its hole. I am perfectly satisfied as the result of my patient and tiring watching, therefore, that the earth-worm can secure its object just according to which method best suits the thing it desires to obtain, either by encircling a part of it with its prehensile head, by pressing it between two expansions of the head-like lips, or by attaching its head and mouth in the way of a sucker."

Prof. Paley further describes a habit of the earth-worm not before noticed by any writer. He had noticed that most of the worm-holes in his garden were stopped up with leaves of the Weeping Willow, which had fallen the previous autumn. On examining separately a number of the leaves placed in the holes, he was astonished to find that every leaf had its stalk end uppermost. The tips of the leaves appeared as if they had been nibbled, or partly eaten within the holes, and he believes that the worms have intelligence enough to find out by touch the right and wrong ends of the leaves (the stalk being too high for them), and to act accordingly.

Worms feed by passing rich earth, full of organic matter, through their peculiar intestinal canal, where it is delayed in its passage by the partitions already alluded to, and triturated by the gizzards it is ground in. When all the organic matter required by worms has been thus drained, the remainder is ejected in those little spirally-arranged hillocks strewn so abundantly on the grass which we call "worm-casts." These worm-casts, however, perform really important functions. Just a century ago, the Rev. Gilbert White put in a plea for earth-worms, notwithstanding the evil odour in which these humble creatures are still held in agricultural districts. Although they are in appearance a small and despicable link in the chain of nature, yet, if lost, he contends they would make a lamentable chasm. Apart from their affording stock food for birds and many other animals, he contends they are useful to the farmer in boring, loosening, and perforating the soil, and in rendering it pervious to rains and the fibres of plants, from their habit of dragging leaves, straws, &c., down into it. We may add that the roots of plants need the circulation of air as well as leaves, and this is most effectively produced by the porosity given to the soil burrowed by worms. The "worm-casts" form a capital top-dressing for all kinds of grass, and it is now known that earth-worms can in this way add considerably to the depth of soil.

Many years ago, Mr. Wedgewood, a friend and relative of Dr. Charles Darwin, noticed that in a field of his, in Staffordshire, the soil appeared to have increased in depth. In some places as much as one inch had been formed in three years, and, at last, Mr. Wedgewood came to the conclusion that earth-worms had been the chief agents in this remarkable addition. This led Mr. Darwin to make some investigations with a view to discovering how far earth-worms were instrumental in the formation of soils, and he afterwards communicated the results of his observations to the Geological Society of London. He found that well-nigh the whole surface of the grass-field was covered with worm-castings Although the casts of the larger worms were the more conspicuous, standing up as little mounds at no great distance from one another, yet they had not, on the whole, so great an effect as the multitude of the heaps of younger and smaller worms which are hidden under the herbage. Dr. Darwin says :—" On carefully examining between the blades of grass, I found scarcely a space of two inches square without a little heap of cylindrical castings." The rate at which the layer of new soil is thus formed may be guessed at from some of the facts produced by Darwin. In one case, in a field which had been reclaimed from waste land, three inches depth of mould had been prepared by the worms in fifteen years ; and in another, within a period of less than eighty years, the earth-worms had covered a bed of sand with soil to the depth of between twelve and thirteen inches!

It has been noticed that as worms desert their old burrows, the soil sinks in and fills them; and by this means a constant circulation is continued, the vegetable mould extending itself downwards, while the "dead," or purely mineral, soil is brought up to the surface. Even in the unmoved gravel of any pit we may see that the earth-worms are invading it, eating out the sand between the stones, and running their burrows in and out and among it. Professor Paley says:—"Seeds of trees are dragged by worms into their holes, and there germinate. This is most commonly the case with the seeds of the ash and the sycamore, both of which have their winged appendages set slightly on one side, like the sails of a windmill, or the screw-propeller of a ship, so that they are carried by the wind and fall aslant at some distance from the trees. I have repeatedly drawn both of these seeds out of worm-holes, after they had begun to germinate. The fact is established by the carrying down of seeds, strewed on the surface, by worms kept in a pot. There can be no doubt, therefore, that it is one of the provisions of nature for the propagation of vegetable life.

"Every effect that the worm leaves visible on the surface seems done at a time when its enemies, the birds, are not abroad. How a blind creature can tell night from day seems surprising; possibly the warmth of the sun, or the dew at night, may serve it for this end. By keeping one or two worms in a flower-pot, I once or twice found one partly exposed. It was passing, by peculiar jerks made, with intervals of rest, from one hole into another. From this I suspected that, as in a rabbit-warren, the same creature has several holes communicating with each other underground.

"To ascertain this, after keeping the worms for some time in a flower-pot, I let them escape, and by drying the earth I was able to dissect it so as to expose all the galleries and passages. I found these very numerous, and towards the bottom of the pot containing portions of leaves which had been drawn down for food. Grains of wheat and other seeds had been carried down to the bottom, and it seemed to me that the worms had fed on the tangled roots which these seeds had sent out through the whole thickness of the earth. The *excreta* in some cases were adhering to the sides of the pot. I think they must have some way of conveying it or pushing it out of their holes, as birds are said to eject the dirt of the young nestlings. I think, also, that it is got rid of as soon as deposited. For, though worms are very shy of making themselves visible by day, it is common to find worm-casts so moist and fresh that they have evidently just been thrown up. This is the case with mole-heaps; but I never saw, and I never met with any one who could say that he had seen, the earth actually being thrown up. The mole, like the worm, is evidently very sensitive to the tread of a foot. Both remain quiet when they feel the vibration of the ground.

"Worms by no means invariably draw into their holes leaves or bits of sticks, or cover them over with pebbles. The reason of their doing so at all is therefore the more obscure, since it is not a necessity. Very often the hole is marked only by the little heaps of earthy *excreta*, and however carefully you remove these, you will find the hole itself is completely stopped. They nibble off the ends first, and then pull the remainder down lower, till little more than the stalk and mid-rib is left. And a little observation will show that the leaves have really been devoured, and have not rotted away in the moist earth. This fact I ascertained to a positive certainty by repeated supplies of dry leaves put into the flower-pot, the whole being clean eaten up except short portions of the stalks. It seems then that a very large part of the decaying vegetable matter in gardens is consumed by the numerous lob-worms, for they are greedy eaters, though they seem to do no harm to growing plants, even if they do eat some of the fibrous roots. In this respect the worm resembles the mole and the dung-beetle, which never leave the hole to the upper surface open to the air, as most of the burrowing animals do.

"Not only leaves were thus drawn in and devoured, but grains of wheat, canary, and rape-seed, sprinkled on the top of the earth in the flower-pot, were gradually carried down, and soon entirely disappeared; so that after a few days not a single seed was to be seen. I tried bits of stick, bread-crumbs, scraps of gingerbread, and biscuit, but they were not much noticed, though the sticks were generally moved.

After a few days the seeds came up, thus affording a pretty conclusive proof that one province or function of the earth-worm is to promote the growth of plants by burying seed which might otherwise perish, or be picked up by birds."

This last little creature fitly closes our list of the chief British animals, vertebrate and invertebrate, which pass all or some of their lives underground. Enough has been educed, however, to prove to us that the soil beneath our feet is no waste place, but a habitation, a shelter, and a home to innumerable creatures belonging to almost every type of animal life. And we cannot but see, in the wonderful structural adaptations of organs to a subterranean life, as well as in the *instincts* which prompt creatures to seek that shelter in the bosom of the earth denied to them outside it, the presence of the creative Wisdom which is extended to the lowest as well as to the highest organized of His works!

PART II.

OUR GEOLOGICAL RECORDS.

CHAPTER VI.

THE GENERAL STORY OF THE ROCKS.

BUT if the soil beneath us is the homely shelter of so many kinds of animals, what shall we say when we extend our researches lower still, and find traces of both animal and vegetable life, which must have been in existence long before the present creation began? No matter how low down in the bowels of the earth we are enabled to go in our deep mines, these evidences of a former life are still present. In the deepest coal-pits you will find the seam of black shale, which always overlies the coal, full of the remains of fossil vegetation. There are spread out (in the most beautiful arrangement, and often as neatly as if they had been laid out in a herbarium) ferns, leaves, and flattened stems of trees. In addition, you will not unfrequently get the remains, or, indeed, the entire bodies, of fossil fishes, although not more than a few inches in length, as in the North Staffordshire coal-fields. Every scale, fin, etc., of these fossil fishes is preserved; or you may find bands of ironstone full of fossil mussels or other shells, which, as you study them, give you every indication a reasonable mind can require that they were really once alive!

Amazed with your discovery of the proofs of former life so abundantly brought before your notice at such a depth underground, you, perhaps, change the scene of your investigations for the hills and mountains. Here you are as high above the sea-level as formerly in the mines you were beneath it. You scale the rocks to get to the summit, but as you slowly ascend you are obliged to notice that these rocks also are full of fossil shells, or corals, or some other remains of life which you cannot identify! How is this? Is the earth's crust a mere sepulchre of extinct and dead types of forms of life? Is it possible that we should actually have no platform for the life of the period in which we ourselves live—including our own physical life—if creatures had not lived and died before us, and out of their living parts formed the limestone rocks of our hills and the chalk downs and plains whereon our cattle graze? What strange mystery is this, that underneath our feet, as above us in the blue midnight canopy, bespangled with unnumbered crowds of suns and worlds, there are accumulated evidences of Creative Power we have never before dreamt of?

Let us settle ourselves to the careful study of these "Rock-records," as, fortunately for us, brave and intelligent men have already done. It will not be long before we discover that the fossils *are not of the same kind* in all the rocks; that, in short, many formations of rock have suites of fossils of their own. We are almost afraid to trust to the importance of this discovery, because the value of the inference is so great. If each rock-formation has its *own* set of fossils, then if we but acquaint ourselves with the leading kinds of the latter, we may be able to identify any formation of rock wherever we see it, the whole world over! Are rocks like trees? Do they bear each their peculiar kind of fruit? The analogy seems very instructive.

Thanks to the generalized results of geology—one of the youngest and yet the most masculine of modern sciences—it can now be safely affirmed that the simple and logical inferences just alluded to may be accepted. There are zones of rock-formation which have fossils, shells, corals, plants, etc., not found in any other, so that we may recognize their age the whole world over! Such rocks, no matter where they form part of the earth's crust, belong to the same period. The result of this simple inference is most important, as well as exceedingly interesting.

The rocks of the British islands alone have yielded nearly fourteen thousand different kinds of fossils! All these have been figured and described by skilled and competent naturalists. The rocks of other parts of the world have been nearly as well examined by foreign geologists, and the results are in many instances very striking. In conclusion we have been able to prove that, before man appeared upon the earth, our old planet had for long ages been the abode of life! Man is simply the last comer—the latest tenant of a very old house. The fossils of which we have been speaking are evidences of the ancient inhabitants which preceded him in their tenancy of the globe, just as the mouldering bones of our graveyards are the remains of people who lived before we were born. Moreover, from a careful comparison of the various kinds of fossils found in the rocks of all parts, the important conclusion has been drawn that this past life of the globe was not a purposeless creation, but the development of a Divine plan. We discover that the first kinds of life which appeared on the earth were of simple structure and lowly organization, just as at the last—Man—is anatomically and physiologically highly endowed. Between these two extremes, the former dating backwards in the geological history of the globe to when the earliest rocks were formed, there is an intervening series of animal and vegetable forms connecting them, thus making the life-history of the world the working-out of one harmonious and Divinely-ordained plan! For not only have the rock-formations their own sets of fossils, but there is the plainest proofs that these formations are of different ages. Some were formed at a very remote period, and others, comparatively speaking, quite recently. Both the rocks and the fossils they contain afford the most conclusive evidence to those who study them of the high antiquity of the globe.

The life-plan which can thus be studied tells us plainly that there have been times when animals of lower organization than man have been successively at the head of creation. Thus, as Hugh Miller pointed out, there have been an "Age of Fish," an "Age of Reptiles," and an "Age of Mammals," or warm-blooded animals. Similarly with the vegetable world: there was a time when club-mosses and ferns were the highest plant-forms; then came an "Age of

Pines," of "Cycads," of "Palms," etc.; whilst the trees and flowers which now beautify and gladden the earth are the latest introduced. In short, man has been brought upon the stage of this planet just when it has attained its highest degree of organic beauty, when its flowers, shrubs, and trees have reached their highest development, the insects and birds their most gorgeous colouring and sweetest song, and all nature has been prepared as an Eden for the new comer!

These abundant remains of ancient life with which many of our rocks are so stored that we may say they actually owe their existence to them—are not *lusus naturæ*. They are natural hieroglyphics, by means of which we can read off the life-history of our world. These stony records are "written within and without" by the very hand of God! Every one of these petrifactions once breathed the breath of life. They "have had their day, and ceased to be"; and now their very remains compose the solid rocks, and are the platform on which the present forms of animals and plants can exist. As we examine the various rocks, we soon learn how they have been formed. We find they are of two kinds—one which contains fossils, and bears unequivocal proofs of having been originally formed as sediment; and another set which contains none of these traces of former life, but on the contrary presents us with decided proofs that they acquired their present characters by the agency of heat.

These two sets of rocks are respectively called *Aqueous* and *Igneous*. They are connected by a third and different kind, having all the stratification and other evidences of aquatic origin of one set, with equally strong proofs that they have been altered since they were first formed, by heat or pressure, or by both. Such rocks as these are usually very much contorted or otherwise disturbed; and they go by the name of *metamorphic*. Throughout the entire world the rocky crust is made up of one or another, or of all of these three kinds. In Great Britain we have all of them, and in every possible variety; so that in this respect few similar areas of dry land are so geologically rich and varied as our own country. The *aqueous* rocks are of almost every degree of hardness and softness, down to mere beds of soft and shifting sands. Nobody can long examine them without seeing that geologists are right in coming to the conclusion they have, in every country, that such rocks must originally have been formed as *sediments*. That is to say, the wear and tear of ancient dry land by ordinary weather-action would cause the rivers to carry off large quantities of dust washed into them by rains, so that the waters would be muddy in consequence. Such is the case with rivers in our own day, and we have no reason to think they ever acted differently in this respect to what they are doing now. We know that "all rivers run to the sea," and carry thither mud which discolours their waters. This muddy matter after a time settles to the bottom, and there accumulates, year after year, century after century, as an ever-increasing bed of sediment. Meantime, all the marine animals which have died have sunk down to rest in this soft mud, and as fast as it has increased, the dead marine shells and remains of other creatures have been covered up.

Now let this process go on for ages. We should then have a bed of sediment whose thickness would depend upon the time it had been forming, and the rate at which it had been formed. But we have seen that it has been composed of the matter brought down by rivers, which matter was worn by weather-action from off the surface of the dry land, so that the rate of sedimentary deposition cannot be greater than that at which an equal area of dry land has been denuded by weather-action.

Is it not evident that if such a sedimentary deposit as that we have been speaking of were to become dry land by an elevation of the sea-bed—a phenomenon which frequently takes place—we should have a rock, more or less hard, full of what we should now call *fossils?* We have seen how these fossils got into such a rock, and we can therefore further rely on them as actually representing the *marine* life of the period when such a stratum of rock was deposited. And thus we note how it is that rocks of different geological ages have different kinds of fossils, and how trustworthy are such " records."

What a new interest is thus given to the most commonplace objects! Every pebble or stone which we accidentally kick before us in the street is a detached fragment of a rock-formation which has been elaborated in the manner above mentioned. The soil we cultivate is but the weather-decomposed particles of ancient geological deposits, each of which has the most wonderful history of its own! And as the formation of one deposit means the wear and tear of others to supply the materials, it follows that deposition and denudation must go on together. We have areas of Great Britain whose solid rocks have thus been denuded, atom by atom, to the extent of three miles! But the aqueous or sedimentary rocks of Great Britain—sandstones, slates, shales, chalk, limestones, clays, etc.—if they were piled one above another, formation above formation, would attain a thickness of at least twenty *miles!* And yet we have not the slightest reason for believing that these formations obtained their materials from any other source than the decomposition and weathering of the dry lands by meteorological agencies.

For the land has always been separated from the sea ever since the "waters were gathered into one place." Their relative areas have been constantly changing, for the earth's crust has never been in a state of absolute rest; and so sea-beds (with their accumulated deposits) have been upheaved into dry land; and parts of the dry land have sunk below the sea-level. The reflections of our Poet Laureate are scientifically true:—

> "Now rolls the deep where grew the tree:
> Oh earth, what changes hast thou seen!
> There, where the long street roars, hath been
> The stillness of a central sea."

It is very evident that enormous periods of time must have passed to bring about all the changes to which the rocks beneath us testify. But to the reverent investigator there is sufficient allowance in the opening verse of the first chapter of Genesis— "In the *beginning* God created the Heavens and the Earth." That verse elicited the admiration of even such heathen philosophers as Longinus—it comes to us now charged with a fuller meaning than ever, when studied in the light of geology! For who dare circumscribe the boundless periods which may be included in this wonderful passage? Enough, surely, to allow of all the changes geology has recorded, to their fullest and mightiest results, without needing to shake the trust of one believer in the Book which he treasures beyond any other record! We do not like so-called "Reconciliations," for they must be untrustworthy until we know *all* that geology can reveal. But, meantime, this first sentence affords us certain ground for calm trust that no actual disagreement can ever take place between the two records, seeing they are equally due to the same Divine Author!

CHAPTER VII.

HEAT-FORMED ROCKS.

WE have already alluded to a group of rocks forming a large portion of the ground beneath us, which never contain fossils, but on the other hand are fruitful in evidences of their having assumed their present condition through the agency of heat. Geologists know these rocks by the name of *igneous*. Their history is scarcely less wonderful than the story of the ancient life of our globe which the fossils enable us to read off. Moreover, the great antiquity of the earth, which we can infer from the study of the latter, is supplemented in the most astonishing manner by the conclusions drawn from the study of the nature and mode of occurrence of the *igneous* rocks.

Down beneath our feet, in the interior of the earth, "there is turned up as it were *fire!*" That is to say, we have the most abundant proofs of the existence of a high temperature existing in the bowels of the earth. It is known for a fact that the heat increases one degree Fahrenheit for every twenty yards as we descend in deep mines. And there is every reason for believing that it goes on increasing. Hence, as we know the melting-point of even the hardest metals, it is a very easy arithmetical calculation to ascertain to what depth we should have to go, to reach a point where the increasing heat would be hot enough to fuze or melt them. *Platinum* is the metal which requires most heat to melt it; but at a depth of thirty-five miles from the surface of the earth there would be a temperature high enough to reduce it to the molten state. Hence some have imagined that within the earth all matter is in a molten state, and that the encircling crust alone is solid.

But the melting-point of all bodies is considerably raised when they are submitted to great pressure. And we have every reason for believing that in the interior of the earth the pressure exercised is so intense that substances are thus able to withstand the influence of the great heat that would otherwise melt them, and so the earth as a whole is even more rigid than if it were made of solid steel. It has been proved that if this molten interior were protected only by a crust, although the latter might be very thick, the earth would long ago have been pulled out of shape by the disturbing attraction of the moon and other externally interfering planets. For all practical purposes, therefore, we may regard our globe as a solid mass.

Still, we know, from the fact that modern volcanoes during eruption cast forth great volumes of the molten rock called *lava*, that there must be places where matter is in a melted state, owing to the great heat which prevails there. Now, it may be the case that the fusion of this rock is owing to other causes than the great central heat of the earth. Indeed, there are many conflicting views about it, and nothing seems to be clearly determined. But whatever be the explanation, we know that there are certain areas underground occupied by areas of melted rock, and that these communicate with volcanoes; so that we may regard the latter as "safety-valves." Volcanoes in active operation are always situated near the sea, and large volumes of steam are thrown out of volcanic craters during eruptions. There can be no doubt, therefore, that the sea-water by some means often finds its way down to the seat of disturbance; and by being converted into steam, assists perhaps the explosive force manifested by volcanoes. Anyhow, there remains this remarkable fact, that active volcanoes are always to be found near the shores of great oceans. The only exception to this rule is Demavend, and it will be noticed that it stands on the shores of that great depression occupied by the waters of the Caspian Sea.

This fact throws great light on the geographical distribution of *extinct volcanoes*. For it shows us that, when they were in active operation, they must have been situated near great and deep lakes, or by the sea-shores. In the very centre of France, about Clermont, there are still standing the conical hills, each with its crater, of more than one hundred volcanoes. At Keswick, in Cumberland, we may still see the old core of the volcano which threw out vast quantities of lava and ash during the Silurian period of geology. Near Llanberis are the lava and ash-beds vomited by a *sub-marine* volcano during the Silurian epoch. Cornwall and Devon have each remains of extinct volcanoes; so has Derbyshire, Leicestershire (at Mount Sorrel), Westmoreland, Cumberland, and other places. Arthur's Seat at Edinburgh is the boss of an old volcano ; the of isles of Mull, Rum, &c., are simply the weathered and denuded bases of volcanic mountains, some of which rose as lofty as fifteen thousand feet, and that during a period so geologically recent as the Miocene. In the Isle of Man, at places north of Dublin, and elsewhere in Ireland, but particularly near the Giant's Causeway, we have the most abundant and overwhelming evidence of volcanic action ; and the neighbourhoods of the places we have mentioned are underlaid by rocks, formed by such agencies, and therefore termed *igneous*.

It is only by patient and careful observation, and comparison of one place with another, that we can understand a tithe of the great physical changes which have taken place in the land we live in. We are so accustomed to the enjoyment of immunity from the dreadful ravages of earthquakes and volcanoes, that we have come to regard them as *exotic ;* as in some measure appertaining to other countries and not to "Merrie England"! Consequently, when we learn that that part of the crust of the earth now called Great Britain is as full, if not fuller, of earthquake and volcanic records as South America, we have great cause for wonder. But so it is. If you take up any ordinary geological map of the British Isles, such as those published by the Geological Survey (which are on the scale of one inch to the mile), you will observe that part of the country underlaid by the older or *primary* rocks to be in places perfectly intercrossed with *white lines.* Those white lines are "faults," or places where the strata have been cracked through, and either let down or lifted up—anyhow dislocated. The surface hardly ever shows any indications of these great disturbances, for denudation has long ago pared down all inequalities. We have these dislocations in every variety and degree of disturbance, from only a few inches to as much as three miles. There is a "fault," or dislocation of the solid rock, which crosses Scotland from Dunbar, on the east coast, to Ayrshire, on the west, where one side of the "fault" shows us that the rocks have been let down to a depth of more than *three miles* below the level of the other! It must not be imagined that these mighty dislocations have occurred suddenly, or all at once. If that had been the case, the heat which would have been elicited from so immense a mechanical disturbance would have been enough to have often locally fused or otherwise have altered the rocks most exposed to it. But beyond a little polishing and scratchings of the walls of the faults, we have little trace of the mechanical disturbance. And so we arrive at the conclusion that all these dislocations were of seldom occurrence, taking place along the same lines of weakness, perhaps only a few inches, or at the most a few feet at a time, and so extending over myriads of years before such a result was completed, as is manifested by the Great Fault in Scotland. It is evident that, if such were the case, the weather action upon the dry land, in eating it away, would be nearly if not quite as great as the amount of dislocation, and thus all surface traces of the latter would be rubbed out as fast as they were made.

The different kinds of *igneous* rocks, much as they may be unlike each other, have had pretty much the same origin. A great deal of their external difference depends upon the rates at which they have cooled down, or the pressure that may have been exercised upon them when they passed from the molten to the solid condition. For instance, suppose we take the case of a volcano like Mount Etna, about 10,000 feet high. And let us further suppose that, on some occasion when this mountain was in one of its most violent acts of eruption, we could, as by an enchanter's wand, suddenly cool down the entire column of molten rock that was rising from much beneath the level of the volcano, and discharging itself in lava-streams from the crater at the top. Is it not evident that the whole of the molten mass would be nearly of the same chemical composition? But how different would be the physical conditions of pressure, etc., under which the various parts of this column of igneous rock cooled! The lowest part would have borne the pressure of all that lay above it; whilst the uppermost part would have had only that of the atmosphere.

The lowest parts of such a cooled mass of rock as that we have supposed would be some variety or another of *Granite*, and, according to the degree of pressure, further up our imagined column in the throat of the volcano, we should have formed such other well-known varieties of igneous rocks as *Porphyry*, *Greenstone*, *Basalt*, *Trap*, and *Lava*. Recent researches have proved that all granite rocks have become solid and cool beneath great pressure of overlying rock. Consequently, whenever we find granite coming to the surface—as it does on Dartmoor, at various places in Cornwall, at Mount Sorrel in Leicestershire, in the

Isle of Man, at Ravenglass and Shap Fells in Cumberland, at Skiddaw, and at Aberdeen, Mull, and Rannock Moor in Scotland—we know that in such localities great denudations have taken place, and that an immense thickness of solid rocks has been removed; for few, if any, kinds of real granite can have been formed under a less pressure than **forty or fifty thousand feet of overlying formations**. The mind has a difficulty in grasping the idea of operations on so vast a scale, especially when we cannot call to our aid more powerful agencies to strip off and denude, than weather-action similar to that which we see going on around us every day of our lives. When we see natural phenomena on a large scale, as, for instance, mountain-gorges and passes, we are apt to imagine that the agencies which produced them were correspondingly mighty in their operations. Not so; for here we find that the most overlooked operations are just those which effect the most important changes. The most powerful agent is *Time*. It seems fitting that we should ascribe the origin of deep gorges and cañons to earthquakes riving and splitting the solid rocks in twain; and people instinctively imagine that such forces have been at work when they see natural scenery of such a character. But in reality, earthquakes are utterly incompetent to perform such a task. The mechanical erosion of little mountain-streams and torrents can do more for gorge-making (if only we allow the element of *Time* for them to work in) than all the earthquake waves that ever shattered our planet's crust. The power is not in the earthquake, but in the continuous action of a much more gentle force.

The strata of the British Islands are abundantly stored with every variety of igneous rock. In Cornwall, the sea-cliffs and inland mountains testify generally to their presence. The very scenery of this charming region owes its character to the unequal rate at which the harder and softer rocks have weathered, so as to produce the surface diversity which forms the base of all lovely landscape scenery. All around Dartmoor, where the mountain-streams have laid bare the veins of once molten rock which radiate from the main granitic mass, you can see numerous mineral changes of the most interesting character. In Derbyshire, where the thick strata of carboniferous limestone are crowded with fossil shells and corals, we may see here and there, as in the neighbourhood of Matlock, Castleton, or Buxton, beds of a different colour intercalated among them. These are locally denominated "Toadstone," and they are sheets of ancient lava which were poured forth from submarine volcanoes, and strewn out along the ancient sea-floors where the limestones were accumulating as calcareous ooze. In the neighbourhood of Llanberis in particular, but also in many other parts of North Wales, we have the greenstone-porphyry which was ejected also from an ancient submarine volcano, but much older than those which disturbed the quiet of Carboniferous seas, for the Welsh igneous rocks are of Silurian age. The Lake district of Cumberland has entire mountains formed of the ejectamenta of a *land* volcano which was active where Keswick now stands, during the Silurian period. Green slates, formed of volcanic ash, are plentifully seen; for they have been squeezed until they exhibit the cleavage structure seen in slate rocks which are undoubtedly of sedimentary origin. The *Green Porphyries* of the Lake district are of a most remarkable character, and cannot be mistaken for other than igneous rocks. At Shap Fell we find a peculiar kind of granite of a reddish tint, full of large, long crystals, which people in London may easily examine in the polished, thick, low pillars which support the chain-work in front of St. Paul's Cathedral. Ravenglass granite is quite of another texture, but as peculiar as the Shap variety; and these facts have been of much importance to geologists, for they can thus trace to these two sources many large granitic boulders which were wrenched off the parent masses during the Glacial period, and carried far away by glacial agency, to be strewn over the Northern and Midland counties. Northumberland, also, is rich in *dykes* of igneous rock. This name is given to molten rock which has welled up from beneath, and filled pre-existing cracks and fissures, or which has even been intruded, like wedges, between loose horizontal strata. "Dykes" of this kind are very abundant in the neighbourhood of Glasgow, and the railway cuttings to Greenock from the former place constantly lay them open to the view of the geologist. But the geological maps of the coal-field are fuller still of evidence of active igneous forces employed in operations of this kind; and the cavities of the basaltic rocks are exceedingly rich in the various minerals of the *zeolite* family. One of the most interesting of these basaltic dykes is, perhaps, that which extends from Durham to near York, a distance of about seventy miles. It passes through part of a coal-field, cutting off seams of coal; and wherever the coal comes into contact with the basalt of the dyke, it has been converted at the places of contact into soot, and even at some distance has been metamorphosed by the great heat into a kind of coke. In numerous islands of the north-west coast of Scotland we may see the dykes crossing the country like so many stone walls, for, owing to the superior hardness of the igneous rock composing them over that through which they run, the action of the weather has at length eaten away the softer rock, and left the harder standing in the manner just described. The well-known Isle of Staffa, with its peculiar columns of basalt, best seen near Fingal's Cave, is a part or remnant of a once extensive sheet of lava which was emitted from the now extinct volcano of Mull, during the Miocene period, and its prismatic or columnar structure is doubtless due to the contraction of the lava as it cooled. At Burntisland, on the other side of the Firth of Forth, we can see the ancient lava-stream which caught up and entangled huge blocks of coal-measure sandstone, and the latter are now embedded in it, fossils and all. At Kirkcaldy we have several bold volcanic dykes stretching wall-like across the country, owing to the rocks they traverse having been wasted and worn away by meteorological agencies faster than the basalt.

County Antrim, in Ireland, is covered for the most part by two great sheets of lava, which were ejected by local volcanoes during that last period of volcanic activity in the British islands known to geologists as the *Miocene*. On the coast-road between Portrush and the Causeway we can see the throats of several volcanoes passing through the chalk. These throats are full of igneous rock, communicating with and passing into the over-lying sheets which swathe the chalk all over the north of Ireland. Where the chalk has been weathered, the harder rock in these throats resists most, and so it stands out from the retreating cliffs of chalk as a small promontory. Such an one is the well-known and remarkable rock on which Dunluce Castle stands. Wherever we note the places of immediate contact of the chalk with the ancient lava-sheets, we see it converted by heat from its characteristic earthy appearance into a white crystalline marble, hard enough to be polished. In the Isle of Anglesey, North Wales, we have basaltic dykes traversing carboniferous limestone, and for a distance of thirty feet away so affecting it by the heat which was given out by the injected rock, that all traces of fossils are obliterated. Similarly in Shropshire, at Bartestree, Lugwardine, a dyke of greenstone may be seen crossing the lower old red sandstone, and the heat has literally roasted the beds into hornstone. At Malvern, Charnwood Forest, the Mendip Hills, Tavistock, and elsewhere, we have the most abundant proofs of former igneous action recurring at different geological periods. Enough has been said, however, to show what plentiful evidence of volcanic action is preserved in the rocks beneath us; and to indicate that nearly every geological period has its own set of records of this kind. Our "old and crazy earth" (as Cowper called it) has passed through some strange phases of existence; and it would not be difficult to show that the soluble minerals richly contained in most igneous rocks, on being slowly set free by denudation, have enriched soils and stimulated and promoted vegetable growth in subsequent ages. The very soils which are strewn over the solid crust, and which mask all the rocks, aqueous and igneous alike, owe much of their fertility to the decomposition of many of the heat-formed rocks at whose origin we have just glanced.

CHAPTER VIII.

PROOFS OF UNDERGROUND MOVEMENTS AND CHANGES.

BUT the mere presence of rocks once subject to great heat, and which doubtless have cooled down from the molten state, is not the only evidence

Denuded outlines of mountains, showing how they are composed of contorted strata.

we have of igneous action. To them, however, we may ascribe a purely volcanic or similar origin. In addition, the sedimentary rocks abound in proofs of the great changes to which they have been subjected since they were deposited. Not only are they fractured and dislocated by *faults* (as we have already seen), but they bear witness to numerous other disturbances of a similar nature. The "faults" are of every degree of dislocation, from more than three miles to only a few inches. But we are not to consider these large fractures as the result of violent and sudden manifestations of force. Indeed, the fact that they occur in every conceivable degree of difference, from inches to miles, and that we can almost intercalate a perfect

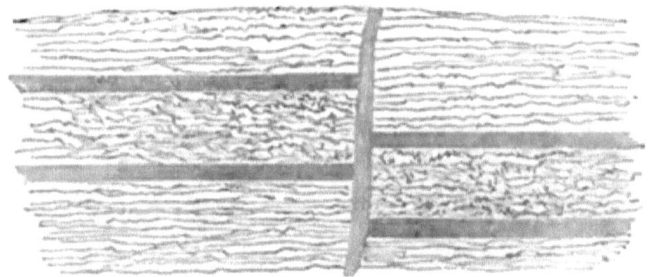

Vertical fault, with fissure.

series, so as to establish a continuity, is against such a conclusion. Moreover, it has been shown that if the more important dislocations had taken place suddenly and at once, there would have been so much heat given out by friction as would actually have altered or metamorphosed the adjacent masses of rock. But, beyond the faintest polish or scratches on the walls of rock

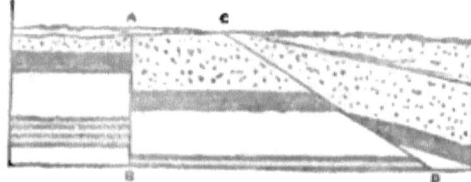

Vertical (A, B) and diagonal (C, D) faults.

on each side such faults, there is no evidence of such a kind forthcoming. From this and other proofs it is concluded, therefore, that these dislocations have only attained their enormous proportions by the gradual accumulations of successive disturbances, which have taken place along the same lines of weakness. Hence, as a rule, the *oldest* faults (those traversing the most ancient strata) are also of the greatest dimensions.

But the solid rocks show abundance of other kinds of disturbance besides the very striking dislocations we have referred to. The young geologist has not long to wander among mountains before he sees that the strata lie in anything rather than the horizontal positions in which they were originally formed. We mention *mountains*, not because these phenomena are peculiar to them, but owing to the greater ease with which the student can there observe sections. For these evidences of disturbance are presented by rocks of nearly every geological formation. It is true, the most ancient rocks exhibit it most, just as we should have expected when we remember that the more modern strata cannot be disturbed without the older rocks sharing in the movement. And so we conclude that, as in the case of faults, one reason why these very old rocks are so much disturbed is that the disturbances have been accumulating during long periods of time; whereas the later rocks have not been in existence long enough to be so much affected. In some places, as in the northern part of the Isle of Man, the Silurian strata stand quite on end, and there are actually localities where the beds have been *reversed.* From the perfectly horizontal, because undisturbed condition, to these extremes, we have every shade of inclination or "dip" (as it is called) of strata. That the disturbances which have produced this "dipping" of the rocks have occurred at different geological epochs is plainly shown. In many places we find two sets of rocks, in which the lower strata are very much disturbed, and the upper beds nearly horizontal. This proves that the lower formation must have been uplifted to the angle at which its strata now repose, *before* the overlying rocks had been formed above them, otherwise the latter would of course have been disturbed as well.

Sometimes, instead of these upheavings, faultings, and dislocations of the strata, we have the latter *folded* in curves of every degree of magnitude, from basin-shaped depressions, or saddle-shaped ridges a mile across, to others so small that scores of similar alterations take place in the space of a yard! Here, again, we find the most ancient rocks those which display this phenomenon most strikingly. The hardest rocks display it even more markedly than the softest. For instance, nearly every part of the mountain called Ben Lomond, in Scotland, is formed of rocks which have so *crumpled* up that you may get small hand-specimens which show the disturbance quite as vividly as if you had cut a section across a range of hills. Sometimes this *crumpling* is so violent, and the strata seem to have been squeezed up so closely, that they look as if they had been *puckered* up by side or lateral pressure. Mere upheaving could not produce phenomena of this kind ; the force which originated it must have been exerted along each side of the district whose strata are so disturbed.

Now, enormous and intense alterations in the position of hard rocks like those in the neighbourhood of Loch Lomond could not have taken place without a good deal of heat being elicited during the process. The force, whatever it was, which crumpled and contorted these rock-masses, was largely used up in the operation. But mechanical force, when arrested in this fashion, is transmuted into heat. And so we find it as a rule, almost without exception, that wherever strata are violently contorted and folded, they are also much *metamorphosed*. The latter term implies change of structure, and this is usually produced by heat, although chemical action may have often had much to do with it as well—perhaps may have even been called into operation through it. Thus strata are baked into *mica-schists*, sandstones into *quartzites*, and entire masses converted into that kind of rock called *Gneiss*. Sometimes the heat given out by these intense foldings has been enough to fuse the beds in places, and thus to produce a true *igneous* rock, which will appear strangely mixed up with the rest. It is in countries where the strata are highly convoluted and metamorphosed that we usually find the granitic kinds of igneous rocks most abundant. Here the mountain-sides will be ribbed with quartz veins, or seamed with streaks of granite. As a rule, all traces of fossils have been obliterated by this metamorphism, and so we seldom or never find them in strata which have been much contorted; and if we do, they can only be faintly recognized even by experts.

This relation between the occurrence of fossil remains and the folding and crumpling of the strata where they ought to be found, but in which, as we have seen, they have been obliterated by the heat, is nowhere better exhibited than in the Silurian rocks of Scotland. In the south they are little if at all metamorphosed, and often contain quantities of fossils, as at Moffat. As we trace the beds northwards we find them much crumpled as they roll over through the Grampians and North Highlands, so much so that they were not recognized as of Silurian age until Mr. Charles Peach discovered nearly obliterated traces of characteristic fossils in the altered limestone beds of Durness, in Sutherland. In the north-west of Ireland, in County Donegal, we have a progressive increase of alteration in the strata which occurs in passing from sandy limestones and white sandstones to quartzite, mica-schist, and highly crystalline limestones, until we gradually find these metamorphosed rocks passing imperceptibly into granite just where the greatest degree of disturbance appears to have taken place. The crumpling and *foliation* of the Cambrian and Silurian rocks is an alteration from their former condition of soft shales, and is to be seen in strata of this geological age in the Isle of Anglesey (near the new Breakwater), in the Highlands of Scotland, and perhaps most distinctly in the Island of Arran. It will be seen, however, that although our oldest rocks are as a rule the most metamorphosed, it does not follow that metamorphism is alone a proof of antiquity. For if strata of any geological age have been subjected to sufficient disturbance, and crushed, folded, and crumpled into the materials of a mountain-chain (as in the Swiss Alps), we may expect to find them more or less metamorphosed.

Sometimes the mechanical pressure will produce other internal and external appearances, either in addition to or, as is more commonly the case, distinct from those phenomena of rock-changes which alter the structure of the masses. One of the most remarkable of these is the change called *cleavage*. It is most abundantly seen in the slaty rocks of the Cambrian, Silurian, and Devonian periods, especially when such strata have been thrown into great folds crossing the country. The *lateral* pressure which has caused the beds to assume this undulatory appearance has influenced every particle of the matter entering into the composition of the rocks. The particles have been squeezed parallel, in lines perpendicular to the direction in which the pressure has been exerted. The finer the grain of the rock which has thus been influenced, the more likely it is to be affected by *slaty cleavage*. When completed, the strata no longer split up into layers along the old and natural planes of bedding, as we see flagstones do, but into the thin laminæ we call slates. All the slates used for roofing houses have been split up in this fashion.

Professor Tyndall, and also Mr. Sorby, have produced *cleavage* artificially, by causing pressure so to act upon clay that it could expand only at right angles to the direction of the pressure. In all cases of cleavage it would appear as if the particles of the rock are more or less elongated in the direction of the planes. Professor Green has shown that "the direction of the planes of cleavage is always parallel to the axes of the larger folds into which the rocks have been thrown." As these undulating strata cross a country in folds, it follows that the planes of *cleavage* are sometimes coincident with the dip of the rocks. When this is the case, the slates will split up more or less in the planes as they were bedded; and then we may find fossils on the surfaces. These fossils, however, are often drawn out longitudinally, or diagonally, or transversely, according as the pressure producing cleavage has been exerted, and the results are the more grotesque distortions of the original shapes—almost as much as that produced in a man's face when reflected from the surface of the convex or concave mirrors which adorn the walls of drawing-rooms. The *dip* or angle at which these important cleavage-planes occur is generally the same for a district, and the inclination varies for different districts.

Foliation is another superinduced structure in rocks of this class, which may be studied in any of the hilly districts where the older rocks occur. It is in reality a separation of the constituents of the mass of a rock into layers of different mineral composition; and it is especially marked where the metamorphism is so extreme as it is in *Gneiss*. Indeed, very often gneiss only differs from granite in having the three component minerals arranged in layers, instead of being diffused unequally throughout the mass. Sometimes *foliation* occurs along the planes of cleavage, and Dr. Darwin has suggested that cleavage and foliation may be only parts of the same process. *Joints*, which are common in rocks of all ages, although perhaps the phenomena are more distinct in the older rocks, are not due to pressure or metamorphism of any kind, but simply to the contraction which results from the hardening of rocks, or when they pass from the soft to the hard condition. When it is due to the latter cause, it will affect sedimentary and igneous rock alike; and so we find joints in granite, as well as that peculiar jointed structure in basalt which produces the "pillars" or "columns," as in the Giant's Causeway. When the joints occur in stratified rocks of value for slates, or flags, or building stones, advantage is taken of them to quarry the stone in huge cubical masses.

Nearly all the effects mentioned in this and the last two chapters are ascribed to one common cause —the secular cooling of the earth. A cooling body is, as every one is aware, also a contracting or shrinking body. As it loses heat it shrinks into a smaller volume. No mechanical truth is more widely or generally known than this. That our planet has been continually losing heat ever since it had an individual existence all scientific men are agreed. If so, then it must have followed the general law, and have shrunk in size. What would result from such a consequence? We can see what takes place when a plump, ripe apple is placed in a cupboard. As it loses the contained water by drying, the external skin is thrown into a series of ridges and folds, which corrugate the entire superficies. A similar result must accrue to the earth if it shrinks from loss of heat. Its skin (or *crust*, as we call it) must also be thrown into folds, in order to pack away the smooth superficies into a smaller space, to suit the size of the decreasing planet. Thus, the great folds and the secondary contortions of the strata, as well as the heat given out during pressure, and the metamorphism, cleavage, foliation, etc., which follow as a result—the dislocations, fissures, faults, etc., and perhaps also even much of the melted lava and volcanic ashes ejected from craters—are ascribed to one certainly-known cause, the cooling of our planet, and the contingent shrinkage of its outer crust! All we have to do is to allow the phenomena to be spread over the immense amount of time our little world has been in existence, and we shall then see how it is that every so-called geological period has been marked by its own set of plutonic and volcanic phenomena, manifested in the diverse forms of which we have mentioned some of the principal types.

We cannot but point out the issue of all this. Having already noticed the wear and tear of the dry land by meteorological agencies, and seen how those agencies are regulated by the heat of the sun, we may now perceive the counteracting phenomena which so neutralize them as to perpetuate the conditions under which life can be enjoyed on our planet. The mighty energy of the sun, exerted through our own atmosphere, would slowly and inevitably wear down rock and mountain until every continent disappeared, and one shallow, melancholy sea enwrapped our lifeless globe. But in the agencies of the internal heat of the earth, and the corrugations produced by its loss, building up mountain-chains and mapping out fresh continents, we have regiment after regiment, division after division, of the forces provided by Omnipotent Wisdom to fight the battle of preservation and continuity. Nay, it would not be difficult to show that, in the long lapse of time, the surface of the earth must be enriched by a constantly-increasing variety of physical conditions, requiring as constant adaptations of animal and vegetable forms to suit or be fitted to their environments. Hence a progressively higher development of animal and vegetable life-forms is the necessary and natural result of accumulating and complexer physical conditions. In the shapes of the mountains as well as in the forms of animals and plants, we can now recognize the beneficial operations of Omniscient Wisdom; not allowing His works to be ruled by a mere succession of events; but everywhere brooding over and nursing them into higher conditions and a higher life, so that one period is but the antechamber to another and a more perfect!

CHAPTER IX.

ON THE CLASSIFICATION OF THE ROCKS UNDERGROUND.

IN the last two or three chapters we have briefly glanced at some of the chief characters of the rock-masses underground, and seen to what causes their origin is to be attributed. We have also seen some of the physical characters by which strata are distinguished, and in doing so we cannot but have noticed how, apart from the evidence afforded by fossil remains, the earth's crust is full of records of physical events such as few people dream of, and yet all of which may be read off with tolerable ease and clearness.

Let us now endeavour to interpret the even stranger and more romantic history of our earth as afforded us by fossils. For our world has a *double* history—one physical, in the story of flood and fire, of earthquake and volcano, with which its crust is charged; and the other a *vital*, testified to by millions of fossils, animal and vegetable, the wreck of former organized beings, and yet the platform on which those which now live and breathe are enabled to exist. It is a strange, eventful history, that of the Life of the Globe! For it extends so far into the past that our arithmetic fails us in giving a conceivable idea of its duration; just as the astronomer's endeavour to tell us the distance in space of twinkling stars only conveys a vague and awful sense of the infinitude of space which would be *depressing*, instead of *elevating*, if we did not feel that it is all under God's care and government! For all the sedimentary or stratified rocks either now contain or have contained fossils ; all such rocks have been deposited along the floors of ancient seas and oceans ; and, in some instances, even on the bottoms of extensive fresh-water areas. The life of sea, ocean, and lake, of all the geological periods from the oldest to the most modern, is tolerably well preserved (as fossils) in these deposits. That is to say, if we could take the rocks to pieces, we should make out a fairly complete record. But seeing we are indebted for our knowledge of past life to the fossils exhumed from quarries, mines, railway-cuttings, or anywhere else where the rocks can be got at for investigation, it is evident that we have not as yet done more than gain a very scanty knowledge of *all* the animals and plants which lived and died and became extinct before man was created.

Still it is really wonderful how much has been discovered in all parts of the world by the patient labours of geologists. From the rocks of Great Britain alone no fewer than nearly fourteen thousand *species* of fossil animals and plants, from all the geological formations, have been dug out, named, and scientifically described and compared with those found in other countries. The German, French, Austrian, Russian, and American geologists have examined the rocks of their several countries, and catalogued the fossil remains exhumed from them, so that a large mass of trustworthy information has thus been accumulated under the name of

Palæontology, or the "science of the things that lived of old." The distribution, succession, and gradually-increasing complexity of organization of animal and vegetable forms can now, therefore, be made out, if not with certainty, at any rate in those bold outlines with which all good pictures are commenced, and which subsequent labours only fill up and complete. We have thus learned that the history of the past and present life of our globe is that of a single Divine plan. For although we may speak of the different sets of fossil remains in the different strata as "creations," it must not be inferred that we mean the globe was newly stocked after some previous depletion. The life-history of the earth, as revealed by geology, more resembles the physical history of a great river than anything else. We know that if we follow the latter up to its source, we shall find it issuing to the daylight from some mountain spring, and forming a rill across which an infant could stride. As it flows it gathers strength. Tributary after tributary rill joins it. Its volume increases as it descends seawards. The rockiest of mountain barriers are sawn through by its mechanical force, and a gorge sufficiently wide is formed. It flings itself from plateaux and forms cataracts; it meanders through wide valleys whose alluvial soil it enriches. Widening and strengthening, it at length debouches into the sea, perhaps with a volume powerful enough to drive back the tidal wave, as the Amazons. It may have coursed from almost due north to south (like the Mississippi), and have passed from almost sub-arctic to sub-tropical regions, and laved banks covered with the different vegetative zones which mark the increase of temperature. But it has been the same river from first to last—from the time when it commenced as a spring to its termination in the great ocean, whence the vapours were originally raised which descended as rains on the mountain top, percolated underground, and thus originated the spring itself. So with the life of our earth, past and present. We trace it backwards to the oldest period (known to geologists as the *Laurentian*), and there we find the oldest known fossil animal. It is of the simplest kind of which we could expect any relic in the shape of hard mineral or limy parts. But from the time when this lowly-organized, primeval creature, the Eozoon, existed, up to and including the period in which we ourselves live, we have an unbroken life-stream welling onward, broadening and deepening as new and more complex types have been created, and expanding now and again into great tidal seas of being!

The history of this life-stream we owe to the fossils contained in the rocks of the different geological periods : not that there ever was a broken sequence in the succession of sedimentary deposits the whole world over, but that we find it easier to classify geological facts by arranging them in a certain order. The different geological formations bear names generally of those localities where the student would find strata typical of the period, or some mineralogical adjective or term is added which conveys some important fact. In the later geological formations, whose history has been more recently and perfectly made out than was the case with the older strata which were investigated in the earlier days of geological science, the names are of a more truly scientific nature. As we shall have frequently to refer to these formations, and the periods of time during which they were deposited and when the forms of life by which they are distinguished were in existence, it will be as well to present our readers with them in their order. Beginning with the most modern deposits and gradually arranging them in the order of their antiquity, we find that the following is the "Table of Classification of Stratified Rocks" accepted by geologists more or less all over the world:—

1. Recent
2. Post-Pliocene
} Post-Tertiary.

3. Pliocene
4. Miocene
5. Eocene
} Tertiary, or Cainozoic Division.

6. Cretaceous, or Chalk Formation
7. Wealden
8. Oolite
9. Lias
10. Trias, or New Red Sandstone
} Secondary, or Mesozoic Division.

11. Permian
12. Carboniferous, or Coal Measures
13. Devonian, or Old Red Sandstone
14. Silurian
15. Cambrian
16. Laurentian
} Primary, or Palæozoic Division.

It will be seen, as above stated, that topographical or mineralogical names are those most in use in the primary and secondary divisions. In the tertiary, the names are of Greek origin, and signify "dawn of recent," "middle recent," "more recent," &c., according to the percentage of fossil remains which are of the same species as those still in existence.

Each formation has its own set of fossils, and each division is classified as above, because we find that on the whole the organic remains are capable of being grouped into these three collections. The oldest, or *Palæozoic* ("ancient-life"), resembles the present fauna and flora very little; the *Mesozoic* ("middle life") fossils are intermediate in their similarity and relationship to the older and newer divisions,—hence the name; and the *Cainozoic* ("recent life") rocks are distinguished by the abundant presence of fossils which approach in likeness living species, and that in proportion as we come nearer to the existing epoch through the post-tertiary strata.

But although the "stream of life" is thus characterized, it is nowhere broken in its continuity. Formerly it was imagined that at the close of the primary, secondary, and tertiary divisions there had occurred sudden destructions, followed by as sudden creations, of animal and vegetable forms; but we now know for a certainty that the "gaps" which are found at or near the close of those three great epochs are only of *local* character. A river often bears different names in different parts of its course, but this does not make it into as many rivers as it bears names: we know it is continuous, in spite of them.

Each of the formations is made up of a large number of strata, which may, perhaps, occur in different parts of England, or of the world, but which comparative geology has now enabled us to group together. Most of these subdivisions bear the local names of places where such strata are to be met with, and so far this fact is of value to the student, inasmuch as the names indicate where he is to go to study the different deposits. Thus, we have "*Llanberis* slates," "*Wenlock* limestones," "*Ludlow* shales," "*Yoredale* shales," "*Kelloway* rock," "*London* clay," and a host of others, which the reader will come across in any full and tabulated arrangement of our British strata. The same plan largely prevails in the classification of the subdivisions of geological formations in other countries; thus the rocks beneath our feet are all systematically arranged. The first scientific effort in dealing with any great subject is always to reduce apparent chaos and confusion to something like order.

CHAPTER X.

THE PRIMEVAL LIFE OF THE GLOBE.

IT now remains to us to tell the story of the Animal and Vegetable Life of the Globe as revealed by the fossil remains included in the series of formations of which we have just given a list. As there stated, the oldest known is the formation termed the *Laurentian*. The rocks of this period are not found extensively in Great Britain. They are believed to occur in the Malverns, at Charnwood Forest, in Carnarvonshire, part of Anglesea near Holyhead, and in the Northern Hebrides. They are everywhere seen overlaid by Cambrian rocks. In Canada, however, they occupy the greater part of the wild district watered by the river St. Lawrence, and the formation takes its name from this fact. No other formation is so constantly or so much metamorphosed. All its rocks have been altered, not only by heat, pressure, and mechanical folding, but by *chemical* changes as well. No fossils have been found in the Laurentian rocks of Great Britain, but in the bands of altered limestone (sometimes as much as a thousand feet thick) which occur along with other kinds of rock in Canada, a peculiar structure has been met with, which some of our most distinguished naturalists believe to be of a species resembling by the limy-shelled animalculæ now living in the deep sea. The fact of limestone bands occurring in this formation is an indication that life existed when the Laurentian deposits were laid along the floors of the primeval seas; for in every other formation since then limestones seem to owe their origin almost, if not entirely, to organic agencies: so far, therefore, the inference is in favour of expecting fossils. But the extreme metamorphism which the Laurentian strata have undergone appears to have effaced all traces of them, except the foraminiferal structure called *Eozoon*. The name is neither unpoetical nor inapplicable, for it signifies the "Dawn-Animalcule." And indeed as such we may regard it, for we never lose traces of fossils in any of the formations after the Laurentian. This "Dawn-Animalcule" appears to have lived in large numbers over certain parts of the primeval sea-bed, and to have there formed limestones by the accumulation of its dead shells, just as coral reefs are now built up by the branches and broken limy parts of dead corals. The *Graphite* or "Black-lead" veins (as they are erroneously, but popularly called) are believed to be evidence of the existence of vegetable life at this early period of the world's history; just as coal is known to be the remains of terrestrial plants.

How long very lowly organized types of life held possession of the seas and dry land of our planet we cannot tell. There is no reason to doubt that the Laurentian rocks were accumulated as sedimentary deposits; and time enough passed away to allow above thirty thousand feet of strata to be elaborated in the ordinary manner. That fact gives us some faint idea of the immense periods of time during which only the lowliest animals and plants were the tenants of the earth!

Of the succeeding Cambrian formation we have a fuller and more accurate knowledge. Here, at any rate, there is no doubt either as to the fossils or their zoological relationship. The Cambrian rocks, also, have an extensive geographical distribution in Great Britain. Besides the Principality, where their frequent occurrence has originated the geological name, we find them in Shropshire, Charnwood Forest, Ireland, the Isle of Man, and abundantly in the Lake District, as well as in Scotland. The hills of North Wales and Cumberland are chiefly composed of Cambrian strata, and those hills are among the oldest in the world, infinitely more ancient than the Alps, Himalayas, or Andes. Their very shapes are weather-sculptured, and the geologist is aware that, in many places, thousands of feet of overlying rocks have been denuded from their highest summits. In Wales, these Cambrian rocks are no less than thirty thousand feet in thickness; whilst in Cumberland they are only twenty thousand feet.

Notwithstanding the immense accumulation of muddy sediments required to make up the entire Cambrian formation as we have it in Great Britain (nearly *six miles*), there is every reason to believe they were deposited along the floors of a shallow, but slowly-sinking sea. In some of the subdivisions, as in the Longmynd group of rocks, we find the strata for more than a mile in thickness, covered with the holes and tracks of a fossil marine worm called *Arencolites;* in other places we have the surfaces of the strata impressed with *ripple-marks*. Even the fossil remains are those of animals which delight to sport in shallow waters, such as shrimps (*Hymenocaris*). In other places we note great thicknesses of Cambrian rocks made up of *conglomerates*, which are nothing more than solidified or consolidated shingle-heaps, and certain indications of such shallow-water conditions as to enable the waves to exert a mechanical influence.

Notwithstanding that our knowledge of the life of this period has been considerably augmented by the discoveries of such careful observers as Dr. Hicks, of rich fossil localities, such as those near St. David's, still it is of a generally lowly organized character. Naturalists classify all animals into *Vertebrate* and *Invertebrate;* that is, those possessing internal skeletons, such as fish, amphibia, reptiles, birds, and mammals, and those which have no skeletons, and in the latter group we have included all sorts of animals beneath the rank of true fishes. In the Cambrian we find numerous representatives of many of the invertebrate orders of marine animals, but not one of the higher sub-kingdom. And, as a rule, the Cambrian fossils are members of the *lower* rather than of the higher orders of the zoological classes to which they belong. Thus, we find large numbers of shell-fish, but they belong chiefly to that very lowly-organized group called *Brachiopoda*. Varieties of these " arm-footed" shell-fish are still living, but very sparsely, both in species and individuals. But in the primitive seas of the globe they were populous everywhere, often completely covering the sea-floor, and actually forming thick masses of limestone by the accumulation of their dead shells! Thus we have one well-marked subdivision of the Cambrian formation at Tremadoc called the "Lingula Flags," simply because the surfaces of the strata are literally strewn with the remains of one genus of brachiopods called *Lingula*. Others of the same kind abound, under the names of *Obolella*, *Leptæna*, *Orthis*, &c. Among crustaceans (the class to which our lobsters and crabs belong), there were not then living any creatures corresponding to the latter. But during the Cambrian and Silurian periods there were immense crowds of a *lower* order, called *Trilobites*, from the three-lobed arrangement of the hard, but movable segments (like an ancient coat of mail) which covered their bodies. These trilobites appear to have crawled about on the sea-floor, feeding in and among the black mud. Some of them (found near St. David's) reached as much as two feet in length, but this was quite an exceptional size among trilobites, and these big ones have been called *Paradoxides*. Usually they were very small, many not being larger than a pea, especially those most lowly organized, which were usually *eyeless*, such as *Agnostus*. Other trilobites, as *Olenus*, *Calymene*, *Ogygia*, &c., were of higher organization, and possessed compound eyes, which were arranged in halfmoon-shaped masses on either side the large plate which covered the head. Sometimes we get fossil trilobites which even show the holes left in the ridged, semilunate eye masses, where the eye-facets were once. The possession of *eyes* is important evidence, as Dean Buckland long ago showed in his " Bridgewater Treatise," that by this time the adjustment of light to the eye, and of the eye to light, had been effected. Atmospherical conditions of refraction, &c., must have been the same then as now. Moreover, we infer that the trilobites could not have lived at the bottom of a very deep sea, or their eyes would have been of no use to them. For where crustacea are found living in the abysmal depths of the seas at the present time, they are usually found *eyeless*. Some of the trilobites could roll themselves up into a ball (like the common " Wood louse," to which they are in reality nearly related), and in this condition we frequently find them fossilized both in the Cambrian and Silurian formations.

Genuine fossil mollusca of even the highest types are, however, found in the Cambrian rocks, notably near St. David's, in the Tremadoc slates. Here fossils called **Orthoceras** are found, and we know they belong to the same class as the Nautilus of our own days, the difference being in shape rather than structure and organization. Univalve and bivalve shell-fish, star-fish, and encrinites (stemmed and jointed animals, allied to star-fish) are met with in the same beds ; so that the representative list of such invertebrate animals as have left behind them evidences of their former existence, in the shape of hard, durable parts, is not meagre.

At Bray Head, near Dublin, and in various places in Wicklow, a remarkable and very elegantly-shaped zoophyte has been abundantly found. It was named *Oldhamia*, after a celebrated geologist recently deceased. The *Oldhamia* were zoophytes perhaps allied to the " Sea-firs " (*Sertularia*), now so plentiful in the shallow parts of all modern seas. Other zoophytes, called *Dictyonema*, have been met with in the Cambrian rocks in the Malverns, where the latter have been called "Dictyonema Shales," from the profusion of this fossil. Fossil sea-weeds (*Palæochorda*) of several species have also been found in the Cambrian strata.

The Silurian formation is about six thousand feet in thickness, now that Professor Sedgwick's division between it and the Cambrian has been generally adopted. Its strata are more diversified in mineral characters than those of the latter, and are consequently more interesting to the geologist. Besides, this difference in the mineral characters of the strata implies a corresponding difference in the physical conditions of the ancient sea-floors along which they were deposited, and therefore leads us to expect a greater variety of animal life-forms. In this we are not disappointed. The Silurian rocks, and especially the limestones, are literally *crowded* with fossils; whilst the shales are frequently impressed with similar organic remains. As might be expected, the different strata of this formation go by the names of places where they crop out and exhibit their various characters. We find the chief places are in Denbighshire, Woolhope, Coniston and Stockdale, Wenlock, Dudley, Aymestry, Ludlow, Bannisdale, and Kirby Moor, in Westmoreland. All the strata, grits, shales, and limestones indicate that they were deposited continuously, but slowly, over the subsiding area of the sea-bed. In the West of Ireland we have *conglomerates*, but they are so metamorphosed, pebbles and boulders, and the matrix in which they were imbedded all together, that it is sometimes difficult to distinguish them. The limestones of the Silurian formation are often nothing more than ancient *coral reefs*, and their abundant occurrence is another proof of the subsidence which was slowly going on in all the oceanic areas of that period; for it is a fact in physical geography that modern Barrier and Atoll reefs can only be formed where the sea-floor is sinking. Wenlock Edge, in Shropshire, is an old Silurian coral reef; and at the Wren's Nest, Dudley, you may see the greater part of another. A coral reef does not necessarily imply there are nothing but corals; indeed, a reef seems a gathering-ground for many kinds of marine animals, shell-fish, zoophytes, sea-lilies, starfish, worms, &c., and we often see them all fossilized in one mass together. Both at Wenlock and Dudley you get the most lovely fossil corals, whose structure can be plainly seen if slices of the limestone are cut properly. Most of them are reef-builders, although there are frequently found other corals, such as *Omphyma*, which were probably not so. Among the commonest of the fossil reef-building corals of the Silurian period are *Favosites Gothlandica* and *Polymorpha, Stauria astræformis, Heliolites, Halysites catenulatus* (so abundant as to be popularly known as the "Chain coral"), and many others.

Now we know that reef-building corals are very sensitive to cold. They cannot live where the winter temperature of the sea is lower than sixty-two degrees, and so we rarely find them distributed outside the zones of the tropics. But during the Silurian epoch they were not only abundant in our own latitudes, but even in those of the Arctic regions; for they have been repeatedly found by Arctic voyagers in the limestones which crop out from beneath the thick ice and snow sheets of those desolate tracts. Hence we see here an evidence of a great difference between the climate of the northern hemisphere now and then.

The sea-lilies (*Encrinites*), which were rooted to the bottom of the sea-bed at this time, grew there

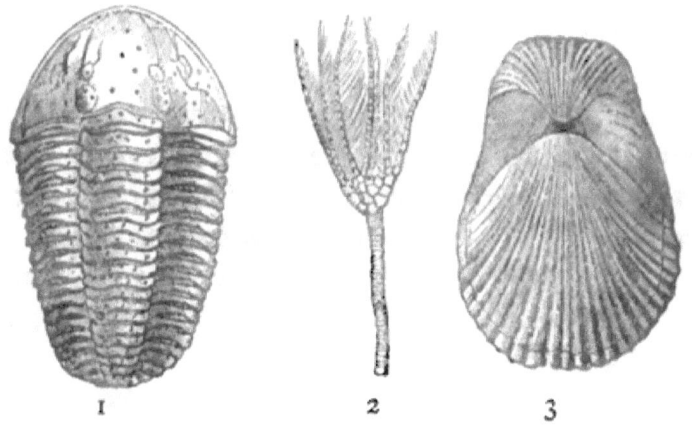

FOSSILS FROM THE SILURIAN FORMATION.

1. *Calymene* (a Trilobite).   2. Sea-lily or Encrinite.
3. *Pentamerus* (a brachiopod shell).

in groves. Very beautiful and flower-like are these echinoderm animals, even in the fossil state, and they must therefore have been exceedingly lovely when alive. We have seen numbers of them, stems, bodies, and the jointed fingers or antennæ, which are so petal-like, fossilized in groups in the slates near Llangollen. The chief of the Silurian encrinites are *Periechocrinus*, *Actinocrinus*, &c. The names of the fossil star-fishes, exhumed from the Silurian rocks of Shropshire and North Wales, show their antiquity. They are *Palæaster* ("Ancient Star-fish"), *Protaster* ("First Star-fish"), and the like.

Trilobites abounded more than ever, and on the whole they were of higher organization. Certainly there was a much greater variety in external shape than during the Cambrian epoch. Although some of the characteristic generic forms of the latter lived on into the Silurian period, the latter was distinguished by well-marked genera of its own, which are to be found in all or most of the true Silurian rocks. Among them are *Calymene Blumenbachii* (so abundant in the Silurian limestones at Dudley that it has long gone by the name of the "Dudley Locust"), *Encrinurus*, *Homalonotus*, *Phacops*, *Illænus*, &c. Heads and tails, just as they moulted, are profusely scattered over the surfaces of the flags, shales, and limestone slabs.

But of all the fossils the lowly-organized shell-fish of the *Brachiopod* family are unquestionably the most abundant. You find them everywhere, but particularly in the limestones; the univalve, bivalve, and *Cephalopodous* ("head-footed," as Nautilus) mollusca being usually most plentiful in the shales and slates. Some rocks appear to be almost wholly composed of brachiopods, especially of two abundant genera, *Pentamerus* and *Rhynchonella*. In Shropshire the former genus has given the name of "Pentamerus beds" to one zone of rock; and in the Woolhope beds several species of this fossil occur by millions. Besides these we have such characteristic Silurian genera as *Atrypa, Orthis, Strophomena, Leptæna*, &c. The true mollusca are commoner in the Silurian rocks than in the Cambrian. Sometimes (as in the slates quarried near Llangollen, and which belong to the Upper Silurian period) you find incalculable numbers of them covering the surfaces of the slabs or slates. At the place just mentioned you meet with a bivalve mollusk (*Cardiola*)—or rather the *cast* of it, for all the lime of the shells has been dissolved away—with the two valves opened out, but still in contact at the hinge. A higher type of mollusk, that related to the cuttle-fishes and nautilus, is abundantly present in the same strata. It is called *Orthoceras primævum*, and has a very wide distribution in the Silurian rocks of the British islands. Near Kendal we find in the uppermost and latest-formed strata of the Silurian age large numbers of bivalve shells, such as *Avicula, Orthonota*, and *Pterinea*.

The *Orthoceras*, or nautilus type of mollusk, is unquestionably the most highly organized, from a zoological point of view, of any found in the Silurian rocks. A great many external types of it had by this time been introduced, such as *Lituites, Phragmoceras*, &c. Of single-shelled (univalve) mollusca, the most characteristic perhaps is the lovely *Murchisonia* (named after the great geological explorer of the Silurian system), and species of *Euomphalus, Bellerophon*, &c.

Frequently, in the black and softer shales, in many places in Shropshire, North Wales, and about Windermere, as well as at Moffat and near Dumfries in Scotland, we find the most profuse abundance of peculiar kinds of zoophytes called *Graptolites*. Many of them are converted into iron-pyrites, and therefore look as if they had been electrotyped or gilded on the surface of the shales. They are very interesting and beautiful fossils. The beds which contain them plentifully often go by the name of "Graptolite Shales."

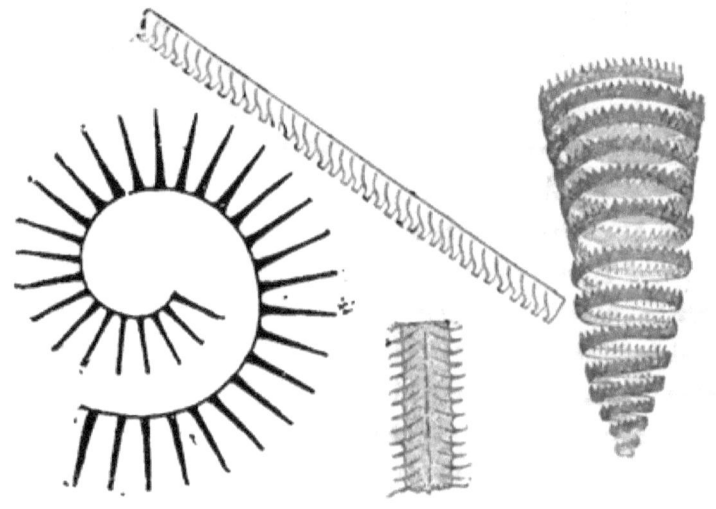

Various Species of Graptolites.

Towards the close of this period crustacea of other types appeared on the stage of creation—huge crustaceans, having lobster-like affinities. Some of them were as much as five or six feet in length, and the strata in which they are most abundant are found near Ludlow, at Aymestry, Downton, and Ledbury. The names of these huge lobster-like fossil creatures are *Pterygotus*, *Eurypterus*, *Slimonia*, Some of the latter have been met with in the upper Silurian rocks of Scotland in a nearly perfect condition.

But by far the most important event towards the

and of the Silurian epoch was the *appearance of Fishes!* We have not met with any trace of them before, and now we come upon them under strange circumstances. They are of two kinds,—one group evidently preyed upon by the other. Offence and defence are plainly read off in their structures. The first is named *Onchus*, and from its back-spine we know it belonged to the predatory class of which the modern Dog-fish is an example. *Pteraspis* is the name of the *defended* fish, covered with bony plates like a stong armour, although not a large fish. Near Ludlow is a thin bed about four inches in thickness, which can, however, be traced for miles, full of the remains of these early fishes; and it is known among geologists as the "Bone-bed." It is about this time, also, that we get the first traces of *Land-vegetation*, and we never lose sight of it afterwards, upwards and onwards to our own day. These first fossil vegetables are the spore-cases of a club-moss called *Pachytheca sphærica*.

The "Ledbury Shales" and "Downton Sandstones" are regarded as *Passage-beds* between the Silurian and Devonian formations. Through them, in the west of England, they pass one into the other, apparently without break of continuity. In these beds we find an abundance of the remains of the gigantic crustaceans. Sometimes parts of these rocks are called "Tilestones," that being the local name for them, derived from their use.

The Devonian, or Old Red Sandstone, is a most interesting and instructive geological formation on many accounts. Those who have read the late Hugh Miller's charming book on it will ever afterwards turn towards it with something of affectionate geological respect. But the lessons which its fossil remains teach respecting the upwards and onwards development of life which was then taking place, constitute its real interest. As a formation we may regard the two names as being given to the marine and the lacustrine strata respectively. *Devonian* is used when speaking of the former; *Old Red Sandstone* when referring to the latter. Thus we have evidence not only of long-continued marine deposition, but also of the existence of fresh-water lakes in what is now Ireland and Scotland, as extensive as those which now chequer the map of North America. The fossils in these two sets of strata are quite different. The marine strata are found chiefly in Devonshire, North and South, whence their name; although we know they are continuous with the rocks of the hills which bound the river Rhine. They consist of red and grey sandstones, shales, grits, limestones, purple slates, conglomerates. The shales and purple slates often attain great thickness and are full of fossils which are unmistakably of marine habits, such as trilobites and bivalve mollusca; and others allied to the existing nautilus, called *Clymenia*, as well as the straight-chambered mollusca of the same class as the latter, called *Orthoceratites*. In North Devonshire these shales attain great thickness, and we find them on the opposite side of the bay as well. The limestones of South Devonshire, as at Newton Abbot, Torquay, Plymouth, and elsewhere, are often full of fossils, especially of *corals*, and the latter furnish abundant proof of reefs having been formed in the warm waters of the Devonian seas by these now extinct members of a most ancient and geologically useful set of animals. The fossils which may be deemed "characteristic" of the Devonian rocks are, among the brachiopods, *Spirifera disjuncta*, *Stringocephalus*, *Uncites*, &c.; among the bivalve mollusca, *Megalodon*; among trilobites (which are frequently very abundant, especially in the shales and slates, being evidently marine mud-loving animals) we find *Homalonotus*, *Phacops*, *Bronteus*, &c. A peculiar fossil, believed to be a coral, called *Calceola*, also abounds, sometimes comprising entire beds of rocks. We have abundant proof, therefore, that the Devonian seas were plentifully stocked with various forms of marine life.

A dry-land barrier must at this time have separated the marine area from that where the large lakes extended; although it would almost appear as if the *lowermost* Old Red Sandstone and the *lowermost* Devonian strata were of identical origin. But as time rolled on, and we approach the later stages of this eventful geological epoch, we find the Devonian and Old Red Sandstone beds more marked off from each other, both in the mineralogical characters of their strata and the fossils they contain. The Old Red Sandstone includes no trilobites, brachiopods, or other undoubtedly marine creatures. Its strata are frequently stocked with fossil fishes of various kinds, insomuch that poor Hugh Miller termed this "The Age of Fishes." But these fish are for the most part allied to those which still affect rivers and lakes, as the bony-plated pike, the *Polypterus* of the African water system, and even the common Sturgeon, so abundant in the Russian lakes and rivers. These fish are covered with bony plates, of various sizes and shapes, each plate being usually veneered with enamel, so as to originate the term *ganoid* (which signifies "glistening") for the order to which they belong. The order is now but poorly represented, and its members are separated by oceans and seas

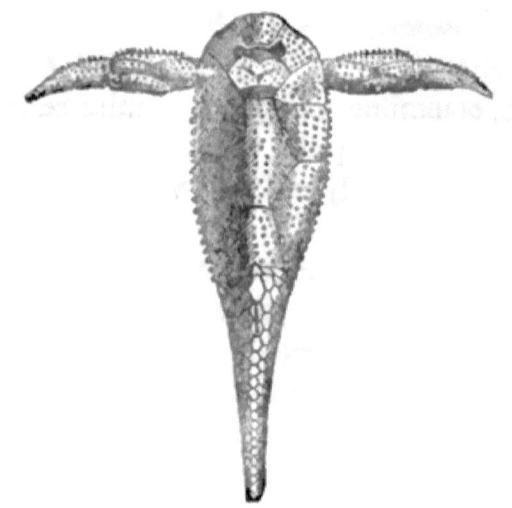

Pterichthys Milleri.

geographically as widely asunder as possible, like the scattered remnants of some great nation whose country has been taken away and given to another. But during the Old Red Sandstone period the *Ganoid* fishes were a dominant order, differentiated into a host of generic and specific types, ranging in size from the huge *Asterolepis*, thirty feet in length (found fossilized in the rocks at Stromness, and about which

Hugh Miller has discoursed so eloquently), to the little *Osteolepis*, so abundant in the dark gray flagstones of Caithness, where their consorted bodies often mat the surface, and their glistening black scales are seen everywhere. In other places there are concretionary nodules, which have to be broken open before the remains of the fossil fishes are beheld. Under these conditions we find that strange fish, first discovered by Hugh Miller, called *Pterichthys*. Among other fossil fishes of this era, more or less abundant, and of which a splendid natural storehouse is to be found in the yellow flags of Dura Den, near Coupar, in Fifeshire, are *Glyptopomus*, *Holoptychius*, *Dipterus*, *Gyrolepis*, *Coccosteus*, *Glyptolepis*, *Cephalaspis*, &c. In the Lower Old Red Sandstone beds which build up part of the Grampian Hills, and also found to so large an extent in Forfarshire and Perthshire, we get huge crustacea, or "cray-fish," similar to those met with in the "passage beds" at the top of the Silurian formation, such as the *Pterygotus*, *Eurypterus*, &c. Even the fossil eggs of these animals have been met with, and they are described under the name of *Parkia*.

How long these great lakes existed we cannot say, but it is sufficient to know it was long enough to have formed along their sinking beds more than five thousand feet of strata! The latter are for the most part red or ochreous in colour, and many geologists take that to be a confirmatory sign of freshwater deposition. This age was not without its own set of volcanic disturbances, as the strata plainly indicate. Sir Roderick Murchison says the grandest exhibition of the Old Red Sandstone of England and Wales is to be seen in the escarpments of the Black Mountains, and in the Fans of Brecon and Caermarthen—the one 2,862, and the other 2,590 feet above the sea-level. The mass of red and brown sandstones in these mountains is estimated at not less than ten thousand feet in thickness. Here, again, we find such fossil fishes as *Cephalaspis* and *Pteraspis*, and large crustacea as *Eurypterus*.

The Scotch Old Red Sandstones often contain obscure remains of fossil land-plants; but by far the best storehouses for these are the strata of the Upper Old Red in the county of Kilkenny, Ireland. There we meet with fine-grained green flags and sandstones, containing such fossil Devonian fish as *Coccosteus* and *Glyptolepis* (so common in the Scotch Old Red). And what bears out incidentally the theory of the deposition of the Scottish strata along the floors of great lakes, we note that here in Ireland similar characteristic fossil fishes are found associated with an undoubted *fresh-water* bivalve mollusk. The latter occurs in great abundance, and evidently lived where we now find it, for its shells are still close together as when united, and you may trace every line or addition of growth on them. This mollusk was a near ally to the large " Swan Mussels " (*Anodon*), now found so abundantly in our own lakes and rivers, and so it has been called *Anodonta*. It is plentifully found at Kiltorcan, in Kilkenny; and on the same green flags are impressed the remains of the most lovely ferns (*Palæopteris*), some of whose fossil fronds are a couple of feet or more in length! Nothing can be more beautiful than the manner with which this ancient vegetation has been preserved. Every vein still runs along the surface of the leaf—even the spore-cases are preserved, and the undeveloped fern-fronds are coiled up ready for that expansion in the sunshine which never took place! Fossil Club Mosses of large size, and Horse-tails (*Calamites*) of equal dimensions, were also abundant; whilst the higher grounds appear to have been even then covered with forests of peculiar kinds of coniferous trees. Vegetation had not as yet attained to a higher rank than the latter type. Not a flower—not even a blade of true grass—had as yet appeared; whilst the highest kinds of land animals were a few peculiar and very generalized types of insects.

CHAPTER XI.

NATURE'S COAL-CELLARS.

We now come to a geological epoch which would have been highly interesting to us, apart from the great commercial debt we owe to it as a nation for its enormous fuel supplies, from its abundance of ancient animal and vegetable life-forms. The Coal Measures, or Carboniferous formation, has had more to do with the modern growth of England than all the rest of the geological systems put together. But it is not with this fact that we have here to deal. Our business is to note the chief and characteristic features of each geological period, and to observe what strata were deposited. The Carboniferous system of rocks in Great Britain includes a vast thickness of other strata than those in which coal can be found. We have, first, a great mass of limestone, formerly called "mountain limestone," because it forms a great part of some of the hilliest districts of England, such as the Peak of Derbyshire, and the elevated country between Lancashire and Yorkshire, the highest point of which is Ingleborough Fell. This limestone is the basement bed, and now goes by the adjectival denomination of "carboniferous" instead of "mountain"; although by many geologists these terms are employed synonymously. This subdivision of the Coal Measures attains its greatest thickness in the Peak of Derbyshire, where it forms a huge anticlinal, and is believed to be more than four thousand feet in thickness. This limestone is often very compact, and solid enough to be frequently quarried for the purpose of being cut into slabs and polished for mantelpieces. Most of the dark-grey marble, mottled all over with white fossils cut at every conceivable angle, which is so often seen in English houses, is from the Carboniferous limestone. In places it is full of fossils. Thus the upper part of the Eglwysyg Rocks, near Llangollen, belonging to this formation, is nothing but an old coral-reef, and there you may dig out fossil corals, *en masse*, as perfect in every detail as the recent specimens brought home from tropical seas by sailors. The stone walls protecting the roads which pass over the Denbighshire hills, near Mold, are built up of masses of the most lovely fossil corals. In Derbyshire we have seen the same phenomenon; and the geological student is familiar with this overwhelming evidence of the organic origin of the very rocks which comprise our hills in the limestone gorges of the Avon at Bristol, of the Cheddar Cliffs, the Lancashire and Yorkshire hills, and of those in Scotland. The most characteristic of these carboniferous reef-building corals are *Lonsdalia*, *Lithostrotion*, *Lithodendron*, *Cyathophyllum*, &c.

These carboniferous limestones were deposited in an extensive sea, far enough away from the dry land to secure protection from the fine muds which rivers usually carry down oceanwards, but which are destructive to coral animals above all things. There are extensive areas where we do not get a visual trace of a fossil in this limestone; but slices of such a rock, when polished, usually show us that it is made up (like chalk) of the whole and broken shells of minute animalcules (*Foraminifera*). Among common fossils are the remains of *Encrinites*, or "sea-lilies," marine animals allied to star-fishes. They appear to have reached the climax of their development in the carboniferous seas, both in variety of genera and species, size, and abundance of individuals. Their solid, limy stems were composed of hundreds of joints, often more than an inch in diameter, and many feet in length. No fossil is so abundant as this kind throughout the carboniferous limestone. In many places the rocks appear to be composed of nothing else than its joints, as is the case near Clitheroe, in Lancashire, and in several places in Derbyshire, where they go by the name of "Encrinital" and "Entrochal marble" on this account.

The trilobites came to the end of their existence in the carboniferous seas, and we never meet with them again. Those species found in the limestones we are speaking of are small and peculiar, and go by the name of *Phillipsia*. Brachiopod shells, however, were nearly as abundant as ever, and some species now reached the greatest size they ever attained. The carboniferous kinds of these shells are different from those found in any other formation. The commonest among them are *Spirifera*, *Producta*, etc. Of the latter one species called *gigantea* is often as big as a man's head, and is so common about Buxton in Derbyshire, and in the island of Anglesey that the limestone seems made up of nothing else. Indeed the *Producta* are at once the most abundant and the most characteristic of all carboniferous

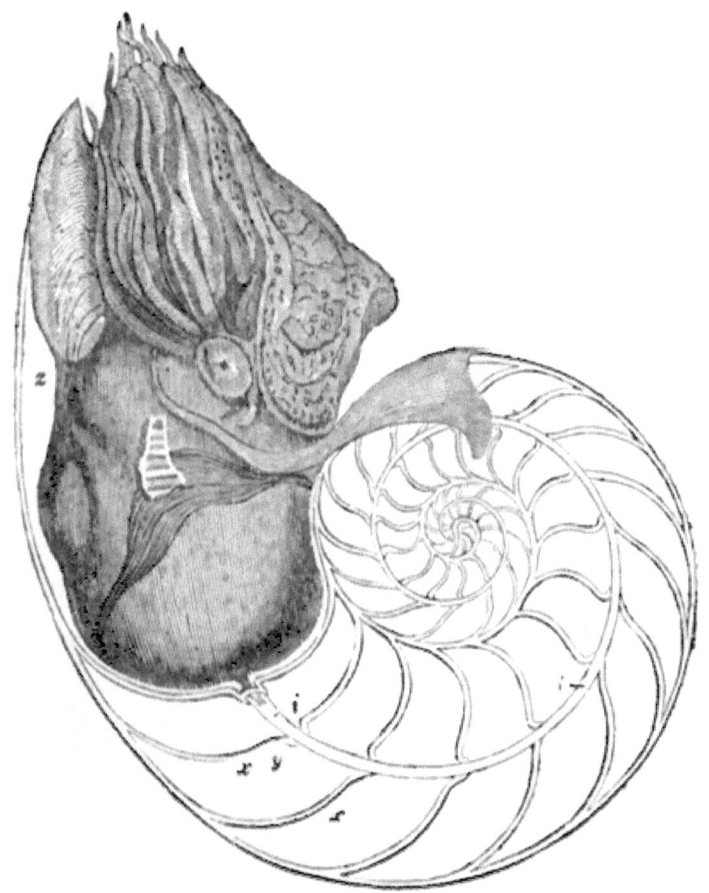

Section of Shell of Modern Nautilus, with animal in last or body-chamber. *x y*, chamber ; *i*, siphuncle or air-tube.

brachiopods. In the lower limestones of the Eglwysyg, at Llangollen, may be seen another species, called *Llangolliensis*, which is so abundant that hardly anything else can be seen. Besides these two genera of brachiopods, others are common, such as *Terebratula, Orthis, Rhynchonella, Retzia,* etc. The fossil fishes, whose remains have been found in this limestone, indicate, by the structure of their teeth, that they probably browsed on the living branches of coral, or fed on living brachiopoda, for their teeth are strong and set in the palate like the stones of a pavement. Among the commonest of such fishes were *Psammodus* and *Cochliodus.*

Cephalopod shells also now reached their maximum of development, or at least some of their leading types did, notably that of which the *Nautilus* still remains to us. Numerous species of fossil *Nautilus* are found in the limestone, some very large, although not so large as the great *Orthoceras*, of which we have seen specimens from Ireland (where the carboniferous limestone covers a very large area), as thick as a man's thigh, and as long as his leg. A peculiar species of this group of shell-fish called *Goniatites*, was also common at this time, and frequently occurs in the fossil state. Time and space do not allow us to glance at the *true* shell-fish, univalve and bivalve, which had become more abundant in the carboniferous seas. *Euomphalas, Pleurotomaria, Bellerophon*, etc., among the former; and *Pecten, Posidonia*, etc., among the latter. Nor can we do more than refer to the numerous "Sea-mats," with limy instead of horny solid parts, which festooned dead shells, corals, encrinite-stems, etc., with their lace-like cells.

Succeeding the carboniferous limestone is a great thickness of fine black shales, often containing seams of ironstone and dark-coloured limestones, called the "Yoredale Series." In places they are as much as a thousand feet in thickness. Many of the Derbyshire and Yorkshire valleys are excavated out of these softer beds. These shales often split open like piles of cardboard, and their surfaces are seen crowded with the impressions of flattened bivalve shells, rarely of brachiopods, such as *Aviculo-pecten*, *Posidonomya*, as well as Goniatites, species of Nautilus, Orthoceras, etc. The upper parts of these shells pass into thin flaggy stone, frequently covered with marine worm-tracks and holes, as may be seen in the dark-coloured flags from Kirby Lonsdale, in Westmoreland, and from the celebrated cliffs of Mohr, in County Clare, Ireland.

Next follow the strata of hard rocks and overlying flag-stones which compose the moor-clad hills of Derbyshire, Yorkshire, and Lancashire, and are known as the "Millstone Grit Beds." Well do these rocks deserve their name. The huge Sheffield grindstones are dug out of their compact beds; and in places we can see the large coarse grains of white quartz which are cemented together to form the "grit" rocks. What extensive sheets of quartz and quartzite must have been denuded to collect the materials out of which these newer strata were formed! In places we get zones of flags, used for paving the causeways of our streets, and on which we may often trace with the utmost clearness the *ripple-marks* left by the tides of untold ages ago. Not unfrequently very beautiful fossil ferns are impressed on the softer kinds; and there are places (as at Peel Delph, near Bolton, Lancashire), where the rock is so full of fossil fruits (*Trigonocarpum*), as to look like a huge petrified plum-pudding. Towards the upper part thin and impure seams of coal occur, and it is a notable fact that the shales which always overlie coal, in these cases are uniformly impressed with similar fossil marine shells to those found in the Yoredale shales. One common fossil is *Goniatites Listeri*.

And now we pass upwards into the Upper Coal Measures, that which gives the entire formation its generic name; although true coal occurs and is worked in the carboniferous limestone in various places in Scotland. Perhaps the Upper Coal Measures reaches its greatest thickness and development in South Wales, where there are about fourteen thousand feet of it. In this vertical thickness there occur at least one hundred different seams of coal, varying in thickness from only a few inches to many feet. From the conditions under which these coal-seams occur, there can be no doubt they are each the site of an ancient forest, which enjoyed a greater or less duration. Of course, this also means that the long and gradual subsidence of the area over which this immense thickness of rock-materials was accumulated, must have been checked as many times as there are seams of coal. Indeed, these coal-beds are indications o the fact, for the vegetation of which they were composed, could not have grown and accumulated otherwise.

Each of these South Welsh coal-seams rests upon a peculiar kind of rock, very hard, but which was once a stiff impervious clay. It is full of the fossil roots and rootlets of plants, particularly of those of a gigantic club-moss called *Sigillaria*, which was one of the most abundant of all the vegetable types which luxuriated during this epoch. This "under-clay," as the bed is called, was evidently once the soil on which an ancient forest grew, the dead trees and plants accumulated there, forming a sort of peat-bog. Year after year, century after century, witnessed the accumulation and extension of the mass of vegetable matter. At length a subsidence once more brought the sea over it, and the fine mud held in suspension buried it all up, and hermetically sealed it.

This, in brief, has been the process through which every seam of coal has passed, thick or thin. When the vegetation was thus packed and pressed, chemical changes set in which mineralized it; just as the decaying vegetation of Trinidad changes into the well-known "Pitch" which fills the Lake. Thus every trace of organic structure was destroyed, except those parts of plants not composed of carbon, and these may be seen under the microscope even when the coal has been burned, by examining the white ashes which have fallen from the grate. Sometimes, when the segregation of some other mineral matter occurred in the changing mass of vegetation, it rescued the vegetable tissues from destruction, as in the "Bullion" stones found in the coal at Oldham, in Lancashire. That particular and peculiar kind of coal known as *Cannel* is believed to have been formed wholly of the spores of the club-mosses which grew in the morasses. The vast abundance of their spores was blown into creeks or tarns which diversified the coal marshes, and it accumulated there after the manner with which the pollen from the pine forests in North America drifts and blows into the rivers and lakes. Fish remains are always found associated with *cannel*, but rarely with pure coal, as if the former had been deposited under peculiar conditions.

Thus was seam after seam of coal slowly stored away—each bed the result of the slow cell-growth of lowly-organized plants; each growth of cell stimulated into action by the light and heat of the sun, whose forces were thus stored up within the vegetable tissues, ultimately metamorphosed into coal, and now given out as *resurrectionzed* sunlight and sunheat by our gas-flames and coal-fires!

The plants which flourished during this remarkable geological epoch were collectively of a kind the world has never seen before nor since. With the exception of several species of pines, a few kinds of ferns, possibly a palm or two, it was for the most part composed of gigantic club-mosses. The largest of this kind of plant is now not more than three or four feet in height, but during the carboniferous period there were various sorts which commonly rose to fifty and sixty feet high, and had proportionately stout and strong trunks. Some of them had regularly forked branches, densely clad with grass-like leaves, which left lozenge-shaped scars on the bark when they dropped off. Others rose and spread out almost like pollard willows. All of them bore catkins full of spores, which

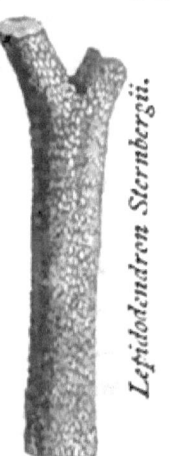
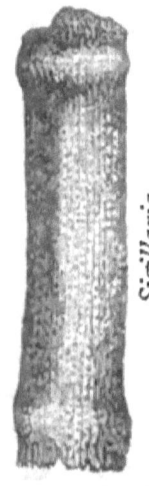

Portions of Trunks of Fossil Club-Mosses (Carboniferous Formation).

Lepidodendron Sternbergii.
Sigillaria.

NATURE'S COAL-CELLARS. 175

collected in enormous quantities, and formed the

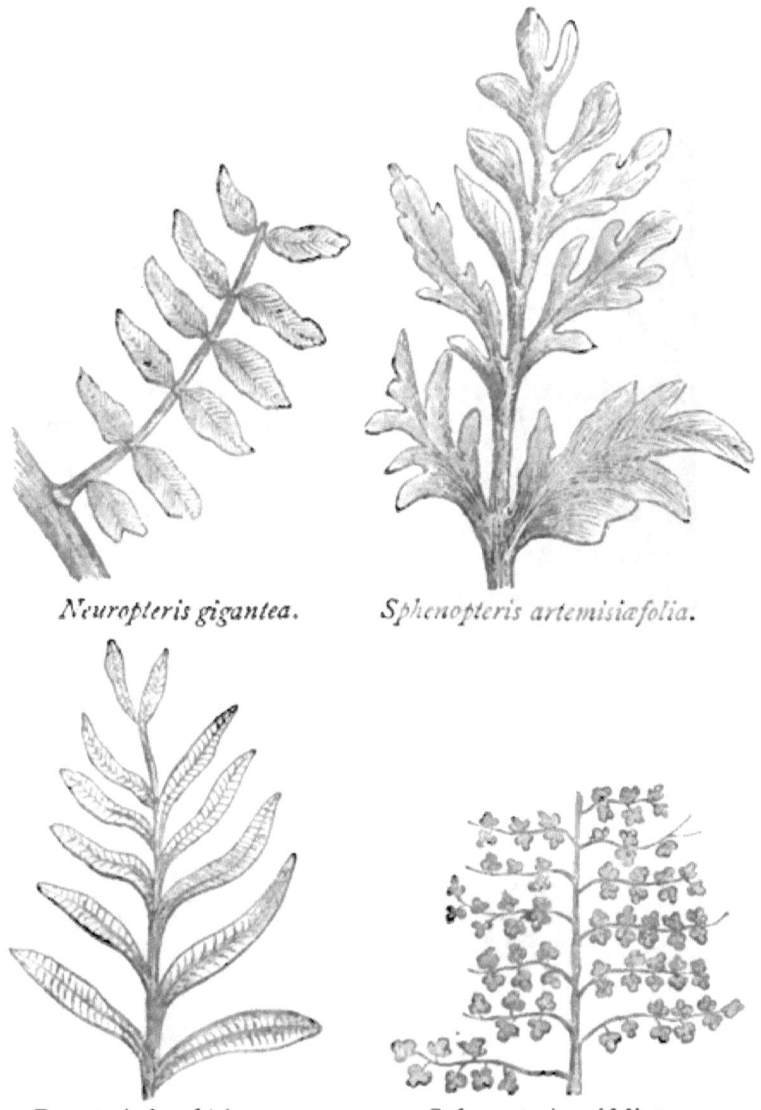

Neuropteris gigantea.   *Sphenopteris artemisiæfolia.*

Pecopteris lonchitica.   *Sphenopteris trifoliata.*
FOSSIL FERNS FROM THE COAL MEASURES.

cannel coal. We get every trace of these remarkable plants — the scarred trunk and branches, leaves, fruit, and spores, all petrified and preserved in the fossil state — in the rubbish thrown out by every coal-pit. The chief of these grotesque and peculiar kinds of vegetation were *Sigillaria* and *Lepidodendron*. The latter was a peculiarly elegant tree. Side by side with them, in the same marshy places, there grew dense groves of even a still more striking plant. Fancy the diminutive horse-tails of our ditches and damp woods suddenly shooting up and bulging out to the dimensions of forest-trees, and you get a lively idea of what these extinct *Calamites* were! Roots, leaves, and fruit of these are

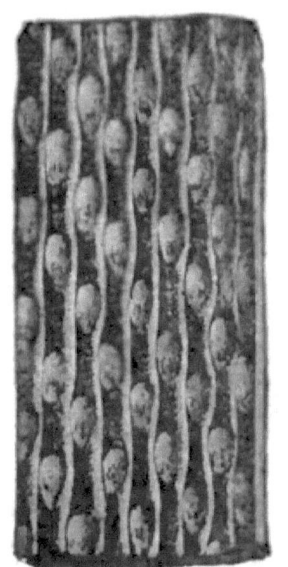

Portion of bark of *Sigillaria*, showing leaf-scars.

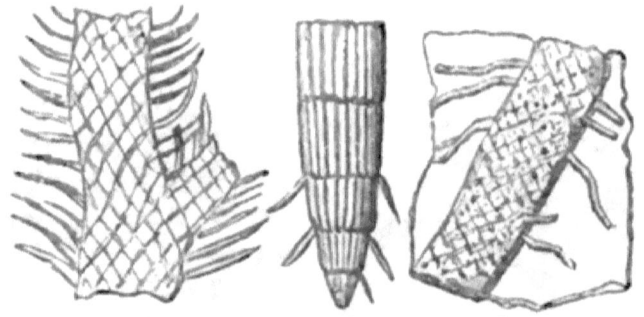

Fragments of (1) *Lepidodendron*, (2) *Calamites*, (3) *Stigmaria*, the root of *Sigillaria*.

also found fossilized. Many species of those huge club-mosses and horse-tails existed together. Ferns of numerous kinds, some wonderfully like those which are still abundant in our English green lanes, matted the ground, or grew upon the trees. Here and there were a few peculiar species of grasses, for as yet, and for a long time afterwards, there were no flowers, neither had there come into existence the insects which fertilize flowers. Numerous cockroaches, mantis-like insects, and grasshoppers had the world to themselves.

The waters, however, were lively with fish, large and small, the preyers and the preyed-upon. The former represented by their suggestive teeth, and also by their fluted or thorn-armed spines, called *Ichthyodorulites*. Their skeletons were cartilaginous, like those of the modern Shark, to whose family they belonged. Their skin was a kind of shagreen. Hence all we now get of them in the fossil state are the dorsal spines and the teeth. Some of the latter showed *reptilian* affinities. Other fish, of the *ganoid* order, were also predatory, notably the Great Fish (*Megalichthys*), and *Rhizodus*. Enormous numbers of small ganoids (*Palæoniscus*, &c.) basked in the creeks. A huge marine newt (*Archægosaurus*) and many other amphibians, of various sizes and shapes, some of them assuming a water-snake-like form (*Ophiderpeton*), and others perhaps that of a modern frog, are to be added to the strange zoological list. It will be seen, therefore, that an advance has been made beyond the fishes, and that the next upper rung in the great ladder of life was reached when the introduction of the *Amphibia* took place.

178 UNDERGROUND.

The coal measures are overlaid, especially in many parts of England, with a set of red sandstones (often mistaken for the Triassic sandstones), conglomerates,

MARINE NEWT, or *Archægosaurus*.

marls, and magnesian limestones. The conglomerates and coloured sandstones form the lower beds, and may be seen in the railway-cuttings near Penrith, in

Cumberland, about Carlisle, at Wolverhampton and Birmingham, at Knaresborough, Pontefract, Durham, and many places in West Lancashire. The magnesian limestone forms bold coast cliffs from Tynemouth to Hartlepool. It underlies most of the area of Sherwood Forest, in Nottinghamshire (from quarries in which the stone for building the Houses of Parliament was obtained), and can be seen in quarries beyond Worksop by those who travel on the Great Northern Railway from London to Sheffield.

As regards the appearance of the strata, the rocks of the Permian formation resemble those of the Trias, or New Red, more than those of the Coal Measures. Their fossils, however, tell a different tale, and at once show how nearly related they are to the fauna and flora of the latter period; indeed, so much is this the case that we may say the Permian genera of animals and plants are almost the same as those of the Carboniferous epoch. *Sigillaria, Lepidodendron,* and other club-mosses still existed, although not in such rank abundance, nor represented by so many species as before. *Calamites,* or huge horse-tails, were, however, very plentiful, as well as several species of ferns. In some places, as in Cumberland, the Permian rocks are said to attain the enormous thickness of many thousands of feet.

The magnesian limestone is an oceanic deposit, and contains brachiopods peculiar to it, and which are not found in any other strata. This kind of rock, however, is believed to have been *chemically* altered since its formation, although geologists are not yet agreed as to how the metamorphosis has taken place. In the limy marls we often meet with peculiar fossils, such as *Schizodus, Bakewellia,* &c., and in Durham, in the limestone, we frequently get quantities of fossil fish (*Palæoniscus*) in a very perfect condition. The first kind of *true* reptile now occurs—a step still further in advance. It was allied to the crocodiles in the manner with which its teeth were separately pegged into the jaws, and it has been found in several places in Permian strata. *Labyrinthodon* remains are much more abundant, but these represent the lower ranks of reptilian life.

In many respects the flora of the Permian period is allied to that of the Secondary formation, and that of the latter is believed by some botanists to have really commenced about this time. At the close of the Permian age a large number of marine mollusks became extinct, although others, such as the *Orthoceras, Goniatites, Spirifer,* &c., lingered on as late as the Lias period. The huge club-mosses passed away, and the horse-tails followed soon after. Great physical changes occurred about this time, which may be seen from the fact that there are few places where the Secondary strata are *conformable* to those of the Primary divisions; thus showing that all of the latter must have been disturbed first. Some geologists hold that the *breccias* of this formation are nothing more than consolidated "boulder-clays," and that they were formed by glacial action; if so, then the great increase of cold may have had something to do with the *local breaks* in the continuity of animal and vegetable life.

CHAPTER XII.

THE MIDDLE-AGE OF OUR GLOBE.

WE now proceed to note the main incidents which took place in what is now Great Britain during the Secondary epoch of geology. As before remarked, the fossils of the rocks included in this subdivision partake of a character intermediate between those of the older Primary and later Tertiary.

The Trias, or New Red Sandstone, marks the occurrence of some of the most characteristic "bits" of genuine English scenery. Only two of the formations which come under the general name of Trias are found in England; the middle division, which is a marine limestone crowded with fossil remains, occurs in Germany, and is termed "Muschelkalk." The lower of our two English subdivisions is in many places simply an ancient heaped-up bank of red or liver-coloured quartz pebbles, and this is abundantly developed in North Staffordshire (about Trentham, and in the railway-cuttings from Stafford to Crewe, by the London and North-Western Railway), at Alderley Edge, in Cheshire; at Stockport, and various localities in the district; about Nottingham, Bridgenorth, Liverpool; and in Somerset and Devon. Professor Hull has given his reasons for believing that these beds are derived from the wear-and-tear of the *Old* Red Sandstone. By the way, it may be remarked that these expressions, *Old* red and *New* red, were originally employed when speaking of two formations distinguished by their coloured strata, one of which was *older* than the coal-measures, and the other *newer*. These lower conglomerates are called *Bunter sandstone*.

The upper Trias, or New Red Sandstone, goes by the name of *Keuper*, a German name. In Germany all

Labyrinthodon (restored).

the members of the Trias are well and typically developed. Few fossils are met with in the Bunter sandstone, for in the conglomerates we can hardly expect to find them, and the red sandstones do not appear to have been favourable to the development of life.

But in the Keuper strata we get many peculiar evidences of the animals of the period; most notable are the *foot-prints*, not unlike the impressions made by the human hand, with fingers outstretched, on soft clay; hence the name which was given to the then unknown creature which made them, of *Cheirotherium*

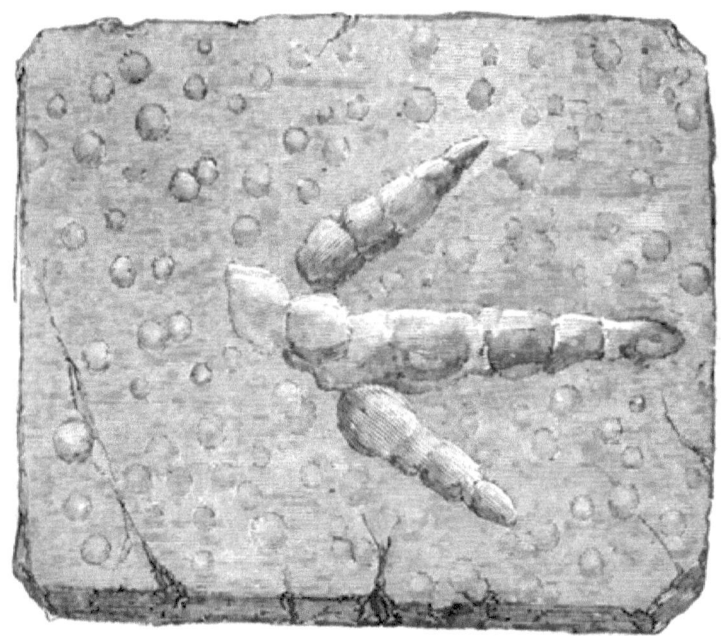

Fossil footprints of *Cheirotherium* (*Labyrinthodon*) and impressions of rain-drops.

(the "beast with the hand"). In the Storeton quarries, near Birkenhead, and particularly in the flagstone quarries opened in strata of this age at Lymm, in Cheshire, there may be seen the regular tracks left by these ancient beasts as they slowly made their way over the ancient mud-flats! You may observe the difference between the impressions left upon the ancient mud by the hind and fore feet. These *Cheirotheria* are now known to have been amphibious animals, and they go by the generic name of *Labyrinthodonts*, from the peculiar structure of their teeth.

The same strata are also abundantly stored with *ripple-marks*, the impressions left on the soft muds by *rain* and *hail-drops*, the *cracks* produced by the heating and contracting power of the sun, &c. The Keuper has an extensive distribution, underlying some of the richest pasture-land of Cheshire, where its marls have very likely influenced that and other counties in their cheese and dairy farming, as well as their apple-orchards. In Leicestershire and Nottinghamshire again we find similar results wherever these strata form the sub-soils. Near Taunton the remains of a peculiar kind of water-flea (*Estheria*), and also of *Labyrinthodonts*, have been found in the higher beds, whilst the marine origin of some of the strata at least has been proved by the discovery of *foraminifera* from the red marls at Chellaston, near Derby.

Gypsum (*sulphate of lime*) occurs in bands in the red marls, and observers travelling by the Midland railway may see the white threads, seams, and layers of this mineral mottling and marking the red sandstones in the railway-cuttings from Loughborough to Leicester. But unquestionably the most important mineral productions of the New Red Sandstone are the beds of *rock salt*, which occur in the higher subdivision, both in Cheshire and Worcestershire. This valuable mineral has long been worked in those counties, as the many ancient towns and villages whose names end in "wich" sufficiently prove. That nearly all the Upper Keuper beds were deposited in very salt water (perhaps *too* salt for animal life to be developed) is proved by the impressions of the cubic crystals of salt so frequently seen. At Nantwich, in Cheshire, there are no fewer than five different seams of rock-salt, varying in thickness from a few inches to 40 feet. The rain-water which percolates these strata dissolves a good deal of the rock-salt away, and issues forth as "brine springs." All these springs are now utilized, but they carried away enormous quantities of solid salt long before man appeared on the earth, and a good many of the lovely little Cheshire "meres," or fresh-water lakes, owe their origin to the depressions on the surface caused by the subsidence of the strata over the places where the solid salt beneath has been dissolved and carried away.

The paucity of organic remains, and the manner with which the strata appear to have kept an accurate record of all *physical* phenomena, such as ripple-marks, &c., lead us to infer that the Upper Keuper strata must have been deposited either in an arm of the sea so salt as to exclude animal life, or in inland lakes like the Caspian, or the Dead Sea, in Palestine. In both these modern "seas" beds of salt are being formed along their floors.

The remains of a true reptile, called *Hyperodapedon* occur in the New Red Sandstone beds of South Devon, and near Bristol relics of the other crocodile-like reptiles, *Palæosaurus* and *Thecodontosaurus* have been found; so that the *Labyrinthodonts* had not it all to themselves. At Durdham Down, near Bristol, these reptilian remains are found in a Dolomite conglomerate. At Budleigh Salterton the pebble beds which form the cliffs of the sea-shore belong to the former part of the period of which we are now speaking. Some of the pebbles are very large, and are composed of partially metamorphosed Silurian rocks, containing Silurian fossils; so that we know these more ancient rocks must have been in the state we now see them as far back as the beginning of the Triassic epoch. The most remarkable fact about these Silurian pebbles is that they have been brought from an outcrop of the Silurian strata in France, and not in England.

Intermediate between the strata of the New Red Sandstone period and those of the Lias are others, less important and imposing from their thickness, but which exceed either of these in the interest which their fossils have created. These beds are called *Rhætic*, from their occurring in a well-developed section in the Rhetic Alps. Both in England and Germany in rocks of this age the remains of the first *mammal* have been found. It was a small creature, not bigger than a rat, but it belonged to a race that was afterwards to be dominant. Moreover, it was itself a member of an order of mammals which naturalists by common consent have placed at the bottom of the class to which it belongs. The name given to this interesting fossil animal is *Microlestes*, a word implying its predatory character, as indicated by its teeth.

Sometimes English geologists called the strata in question "Penarth beds," because the best section of them in this country occurs in the headland of that name, a few miles beyond Cardiff. There the student may obtain any quantity of Rhætic fossils, fish-spines (*Hybodus*), teeth of shell-devouring fish (*Ptychodus*), and those of many other species, some very small, and others (*Saurichthys*) having reptilian affinities. The most remarkable of all, perhaps, are the teeth of a Mud-fish (*Ceratodus*), allied to the *Ctenodus*, which lived during the Carboniferous epoch. It was a large fish, nearly allied to the amphibians, and was believed to have become extinct, until *living species* were actually found in the rivers of Queensland, Australia. The teeth of this fish have been found chiefly in the Rhætic beds which may be seen capping the New Red Sandstone in the beautiful section at Aust, opposite Chepstow, which has been laid bare by the denuding power of the river Severn. Both at Penarth and Aust there may be found plenty of typical Rhætic fossils, such as *Avicula contorta*, *Pecten Valoniensis*, *Cardium Rhæticum*, &c.

And now we come to the study of that great and important system of rocks called the Oolitic. It is important on many accounts to the geological student, and the marvellous diversity of the mineralogical character of its rocks is not its least interesting feature, although this is transcended by the variety and wealth of its fossil remains, animal and vegetable. The lowermost strata were formerly regarded as a distinct system (and still are deemed so by many geologists), and went by the name of the *Lias*. Perhaps no other formation has produced fossils which are so well known outside geology, for the "Snakestones" (*Ammonites*) and "St. Cuthbert's Beads" (*Pentacrinites*) have been the theme both of folk-lore, tradition, and poetry.

The Liassic strata extend across England from Lyme Regis, in Dorsetshire, to Whitby, on the Yorkshire coast, as a conspicuous band of blue and brown clayey limestones and shales. The harder rocks have longest resisted the action of the weather, and everywhere along this route form low escarpments, which

Ichthyosaurus communis, with the fleshy covering restored.

overlook the vales where the softer rocks have been more denuded.

These rocks are usually very full of marine fossils, many of them of such great interest and perfection as not to be excelled by those from any other formation.

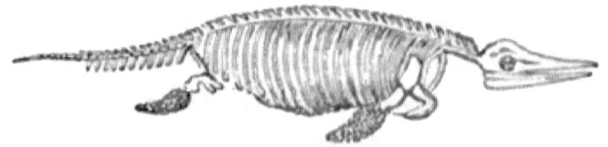

Skeleton of *Ichthyosaurus communis*.

From the abundance of these particular animals during this and the Oolitic period generally, it has been not inaptly called "the Age of Reptiles." For reptiles then abounded everywhere—in the air (as

Pterodactyles, or "Flying Lizards," some of them many feet across their stretch of wing); in the sea as *Plesiosauria, Pliosauria, Icthyosauria*, where they occupied the places now filled by whales and warm-blooded animals of that class; in the rivers as *Crocodilia;* and

Skeleton of *Plesiosaurus*, from the Lias.

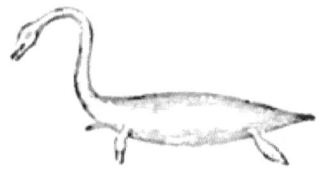

Plesiosaurus, with the fleshy covering restored.

on dry land as *Dinosauria*. The latter were of variable size and shape, some of them exceedingly large. Singularly enough, not a few of them actually walked on two legs (*Compsognathus*) after the fashion of a

The head of an *Ichthyosaurus*, upon a larger scale, to exhibit the structure of the eye and jaws.

little-known lizard, still living in Australia, called *Chlamydosaurus*. The young, middle-aged, and adult of all these " monsters of the prime " are found in the fossil state. At Lyme Regis and also at that great treasure-house of fossil reptiles, Barrow-on-Soar, in Leicestershire (at which latter place the Lias limestone is quarried for the purpose of being manufactured for hydraulic cement), the most perfect skeletons of all the aforesaid animals have been exhumed, and these may now be seen in our principal museums. Some had long, swan-like necks, as the *Plesiosaurus;* others short, but strong necks, like the *Ichthyosaurus.* All of them, however, as their numerous and peculiar teeth only too plainly indicate, were of carnivorous habits.

Fossil fish, many of them also predatory, like the shark, are abundantly met with in the fossil state, especially the dorsal spines of the genus *Hybodus.* Large ganoid fish, covered with lozenge-shaped, bony scales, are sometimes dug out quite perfect, especially at Barrow; such as the *Dapedius, Lepidotus,* and others; whilst the teeth of fish which evidently fed upon mollusks, and which were formed for the purpose of crushing the shells (*Acrodus*), are not unfrequent. Fossil mollusca occur in enormous quantities, the limestone bands being made up often actually of nothing else. Of these the most abundant are the "Snakestones," or *Ammonites,* of which three or four hundred different species existed during the entire Oolitic period. This type of mollusk is now extinct; it was nearly related to the *Nautilus,* differing from that well-known and still-existing shell-fish in certain structural characters of the chambers of the shell. Fossil *Nautili* are also common in the Lias rocks. Brachiopod shells had by this time ceased to be numerous, for they had given place to the more highly-organized bivalve mollusca. Perhaps one of the most abundant and characteristic fossils of this age is that which goes by the popular name of "Thunder-bolt."

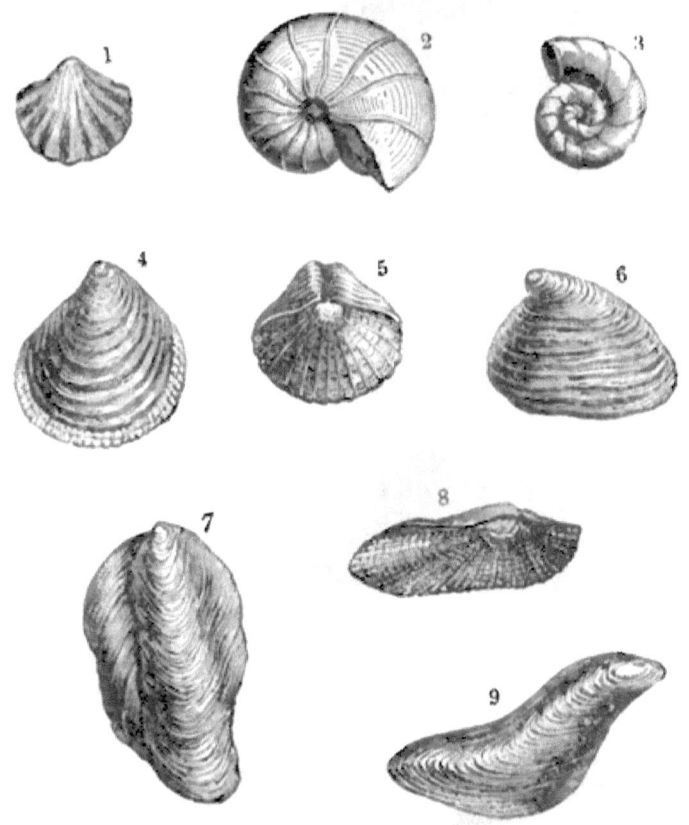

Fossil Shells from the Lias and Oolite Formations.

1. *Terebratula subserrata.*
2. *Nautilus decussatus.*
3. *Ammonites colubrinus.*
4. *Plagiostoma giganteum.*
5. *Spirifer verrucosus.*
6. *Pachyodon Listeri.*
7. *Hippopodium ponderosum.*
8. *Cucullea elongata.*
9. *Gervillia.*

It occurs as a hard, pointed, dart-like object, and is known to have been the internal bone of a peculiar kind of cuttle-fish which swarmed in the Liassic and Oolitic seas. *Pecten, Avicula, Trigonia, Lima, Gryphea, Gervillia, Ostrea,* &c., abounded, and altogether nearly seven hundred species of true bivalve mollusca have been described from these formations alone.

In many places the sea-floor was occupied with groves of sea-lilies (*Pentacrinus, Apiocrinus,* &c). The former of the two just named was very plentiful, and the joints are found in the greatest profusion in the Lias strata. Sometimes perfect specimens are met with,

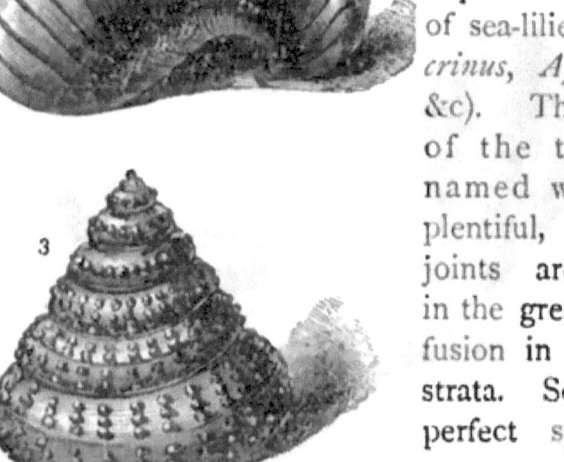

Fossil Shells from the Lias and Oolite Formations.
1. *Ammonites obtusus* (the dark part only partially occupied with dark-brown crystals of Calcite, and the lighter cellular spaces with the same matter, nearly transparent).
2. *Gryphæa incurva.*   3. *Pleurotomaria Anglica.*

changed into iron pyrites, and very beautiful fossils they are. The *Apiocrinidæ* are characteristically Oolitic. Star-fish, Echinoderms, and other near relations of these "sea-lilies" are found fossilized in the same strata.

During the entire Oolitic period the land vegetation was so abundant that seams of coal were formed from its remains, as at Robin Hood's Bay, near Scarborough. In Virginia, United States, very thick beds of coal occur in rocks of this geological age. Ferns were abundant, and many of them very peculiar, such as *Pterophyllum*, especially in the iron-ore nodules of the Cleveland Hills. The most peculiar kinds of plants, however, of the Oolitic epoch are the *Cycads*, which in some sort are intermediate between ferns and palms. Cycads are now living near the Cape, and are particularly abundant in Australia. Fossil insects have also been met with, but as yet, with one very doubtful instance, none which are known to have frequented flowers.

The Oolitic strata (sometimes also called *Jurassic*) are subdivided into several parts, such as Inferior Oolite, Great Oolite, Oxford Clay, Portland Oolite, &c. The name originally arose from the "fish-roe"-like structure of some of the limestones, especially that worked near Bath. Nearly all the rocks bear evidence of marine deposition, and some of them (coral rag, for instance) are full of the most beautiful fossil corals. In Somersetshire these strata occur everywhere, as also underneath Gloucestershire, Lincolnshire, Northamptonshire, and part of Yorkshire. In the Portland Oolite we get "Dirt-bands" intercalated in the solid rock, with the trunks and roots of trees still imbedded in these ancient soils; all these parts, however, being now converted into stone. These "dirt beds" are the places where the *Cycads* are most abundant, and these fossil plants go by the popular name of "crows' nests," from their depressed shape. There are several genera of them (named after eminent geologists who have made the Oolitic strata famous by their researches), such as *Mantellia*, *Bucklandia*, &c. At Gristhorpe, on the Yorkshire coast, the plants abound to so great a degree that we get seams of impure coal, some of them as much as a foot and a half in thickness. In the shales above these coal-seams are a wealth of fossil ferns, such as *Pecopteris*, *Neuropteris*, &c., and also remains of a Calamite-like plant called *Equisetites*. Fossil cycads, coniferous and other plants, are also found in the rich natural museum of the Stonesfield Slate; in Oxfordshire we also get fossil wood, and leaves of cycads (*Zamia*) in the Oolitic strata about Peterborough.

Perhaps the most notable fact in the history of Oolitic animals is the appearance of a *bird*. It is the first introduction of the feathered tribes upon the earth. But what a peculiar blending of the chief characters of two wholly distinct groups! At first geologists were doubtful whether it was a bird-like reptile, or a reptile-like bird. And they have now arrived at the latter conclusion. The *Archæopteryx*, as this strange creature is named, probably had jaws with teeth in them, after the manner of the flying lizards (*Pterodactyles*). Its tail was elongated and jointed like that of a lizard, but the entire body was covered with feathers. As yet only two specimens of this anomalous bird have been met with.

There can be no doubt that warm-blooded animals (which we have seen made their first appearance

The Reptile-like Bird (*Archæopteryx*).

when the Rhætic beds were forming) continued in existence throughout the entire Oolitic epoch. Every now and then we meet with their remains in estuarine and lacustrine strata, that is, in sediments formed at the mouths of rivers or along the bottoms of lakes. Towards the close of the Oolite about fourteen species, of different genera, are known to have abounded; but all of them belong to the lowest order but one of the mammalia, the *Marsupialia*.

The lacustrine strata were formed in a large lake at the conclusion of this interesting age, and they go by the name of the Purbeck Beds. Some of the limestones are so full of fossil fresh-water snails, like those still living in our lakes and rivers (*Paludina, Planorbis, Corbula,* &c.), that the limestone has evidently been formed by the accumulation of their dead shells! The thickness of rock thus formed along the bottom of this ancient Oolitic lake is between 300 and 400 feet, and the area was correspondingly great, extending from beyond Purbeck to Battle, in Sussex. The lowest beds contain the fossil trunks of pine-trees.

CHAPTER XIII.

THE WHITE CHALK OF ENGLAND.

WE have now to speak of a system of rocks the greater portion of which were deposited along the floor of a deep ocean, and therefore they have an extension such as could hardly be expected from strata formed under more local conditions. It is called the *Cretaceous* system.

In the classification of the Cretaceous group of rocks are now included some very interesting strata which formerly occupied an intermediate place, by themselves, between the Oolite and the Chalk. They are called the *Wealden* beds, and they demand a passing notice, if only for the fact that they were originally formed as a *delta* at the mouth of a very large river. As this river must have extended into and drained a correspondingly large continent (all of which has since disappeared), it follows that a good many carcases of land animals, trunks of trees, leaves, insects, &c., would be carried seawards, and deposited in the accumulating sands and mud of its delta. And so we find the Wealden strata are peculiarly rich in evidences of this kind, and we get from its fossils a good, although meagre, idea of the fauna and flora of the dry land. In addition, by the occasional presence of bands of limestone, made up of the shells of oysters and other marine mollusca, as well as those of *brackish* water species, we learn that frequently the adjoining sea drove back the fresh water, and for a time held sway over the site of the delta deposits, to be speedily driven back to its old confines. These Wealden beds take their name from the Weald of Kent, where they occur abundantly. Some of the strata are found at Hastings, in Sussex, and the Isle of Wight. The cliffs at Hastings are formed of the upper division of the Wealden strata, and nearly the same series of rocks may be seen again in the well-known crags of Tunbridge Wells.

Among the fossil remains which have been exhumed is the remarkable herbivorous reptile *Iguanodon*, first made known to the world by the labours of Dr. Mantell. The structure of its teeth plainly shows that it fed upon plants, and it was, in many respects, allied to the vegetable-feeding *Iguana* now living in the West Indies, from which it has borrowed its name. But for *size* we have perhaps never had its equal in any terrestrial animal which has lived in these latitudes. Its length of body, from nose to tip of tail, was about 50 feet, and its height and strength of limb (as indicated by its bones) were proportionately great. *Hylæosaurus*, or "Forest lizard," was another gigantic genus, 20 or 30 feet in length, which abounded during the Wealden period. Both these immense reptiles are among the models to be seen in the Crystal Palace Gardens at Sydenham. Their bones and teeth have been most abundantly found in a quarry at Whiteman's Green, near Crichfield. Some of the *Iguanodon* left their footprints on the soft mud, and accordingly we find them preserved to us, as in the Horsham stone worked near Itchfield, West Grinstead, where also we find the same feet-impressed slabs marked with *ripples*. *Megalosaurus* was also a huge terrestrial reptile living during this period. These peculiar reptiles have been included in an order called *Deinosauria*. Many of them pos-

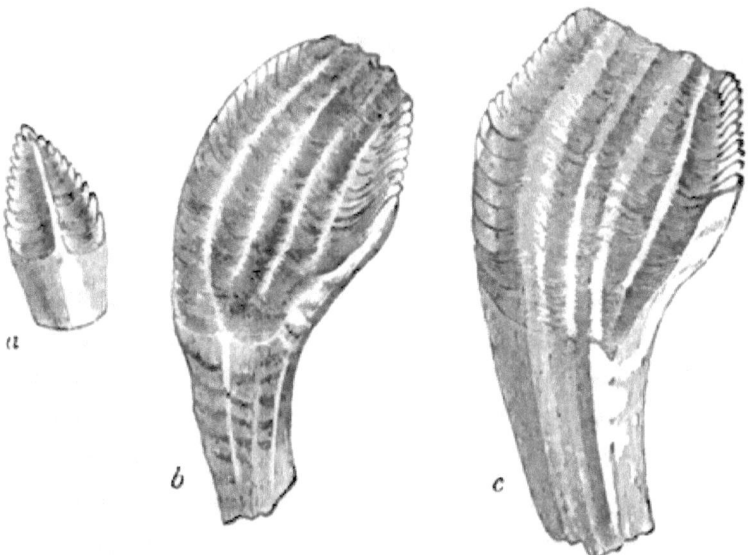

Teeth of *Iguanodon*. *a*, Young Teeth ; *b*, *c*, Worn ditto.

sessed remarkable bird-like relationships. Thus the *Iguanodon* had very small and weak fore-limbs, quite out of proportion with the massive development of the hind-limbs. The footprints of the *Iguanodon* have been found in the Hastings sand-beds at Cuckfield, in Sussex, and these were always noticed to be tridactyle—that is, made by three toes only. These tridactyle footprints were found only in pairs, and now that the fore-limbs of the *Iguanodon* are known to have been weakly developed it is believed that this reptile, huge as it was, walked temporarily or permanently on its hind legs, and so far presented a marked affinity to the Birds.

The vegetation of this time was still largely made up of ferns, pines, and cycads, but as yet no signs of true flowers. Insect life had been largely developed, as is found from the abundance and variety of fossil insects found in the Purbeck beds; but they were none of them butterflies or bees. Most of the other orders of insects had been created, but the latter only appeared when flowers came in.

In succeeding order we now come to a series of rocks termed " Neocomian" (from their being largely developed in the neighbourhood of Neufchatel, in Switzerland). They include, in reality the Wealden subdivision, as well as strata formed at Speeton, Punfield, Tealby, and the beds which have long been known to geologists by the name of Greensand. They are full of marine fossils, among which are peculiar and characteristic species of *Ammonites* and *Belemnites*, as well as modifications of the *Ammonite* type of Cephalopod, with the shells very curiously twisted about; such as *Ancyloceras, Turrilites, Hamites,* &c. The abundance of *Ichthyosaurian* bones shows us that these marine reptiles still swarmed in the seas. In the " Lower Greensand," which is found cropping out at many places in Wiltshire, Berkshire, Bedfordshire, and elsewhere, the strata are often full of fossils. Thus at Farringdon we find a rock full of fossil sponges of various kinds, all beautifully preserved. At several places in Bedfordshire the remains of fish, reptiles, and shells almost compose one stratum about 2 feet thick, and these fossils have been somehow converted into phosphate of lime, so that the bed containing them is profitably worked, the fossils dug out and ground into fine powder, and otherwise prepared as an artificial manure for fertilizing the soils. It should be stated, however, that these fossils are nearly all derivate, and have been washed out of the older Oolitic beds.

The lower part of the cliffs at Hunstanton are formed of a pudding-stone, which was in great request among our Anglo-Saxon ancestors for the manufacture of their querns or handmills. The strata extend beneath the Prince of Wales's estate at Sandringham, and on to Lynn. All over this district they go by the name of "Car-stone." In Sussex and elsewhere we have a well-known geological stratum called *Gault*, which in many places, as about Folkestone, abounds in fossils so well preserved that the iridescent "mother-of-pearl" lustre still glistens on Ammonites and Turrilites. This bed may always be known by the presence of certain fossils, such as *Ammonites lautus, Inoceramus sulcatus*, and *Belemnites minimus;* and thus it has been identified with the "red chalk" which crops out in the Hunstanton cliffs, on the Norfolk coast, where its colour makes that part such a splendid landmark at sea. The gault clay is 100 feet thick at Folkestone. We find it also well developed in the Isle of Wight, Dorsetshire, Wiltshire, and Cambridgeshire; whilst in a deep well-boring it was found underneath the city of Norwich at a depth of more than 1,100 feet beneath the white chalk.

The "Upper Greensand" consists of greenish-grey sand and sandstone. It is often seen cropping out all round the area occupied by the Wealden; and may be known by certain fossils, such as *Pecten quinquecostatus* (or "five-ribbed" Pecten), *Pecten quadricostatus* (or "four-ribbed" Pecten), &c. In the Isle of Wight the Upper Greensand is familiar to visitors from its occurring at Shanklin. We also find its strata cut through by the Great South-Western railway, all about Chard and Honiton; and in the Great Western about Wantage and Wallingford; at Didcot Junction, Woolstone, and elsewhere in Oxfordshire. The "Coprolitic" beds of Cambridgeshire probably occur in this formation. It is well known and much sought after in certain localities by well-borers, on account of its being usually saturated with water which has

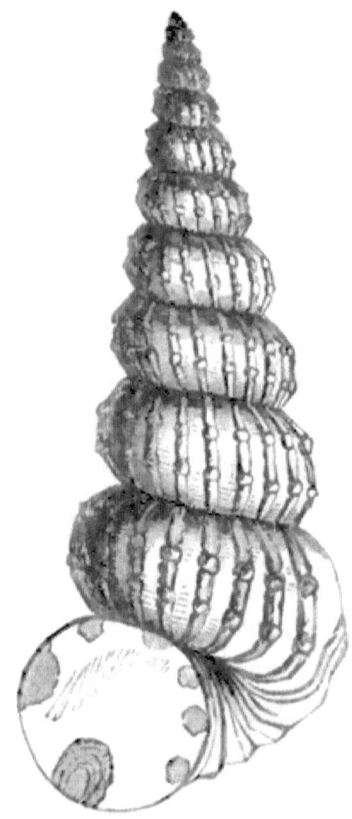

Spiral Cephalopod (*Turrilites*).
Lower Cretaceous Formation.

percolated along its porous strata from its outcrop at the surface.

The true *Chalk* follows, in successive order, the Upper Greensand ; and we come now to a stratum which presents all the characters of a deep-sea or

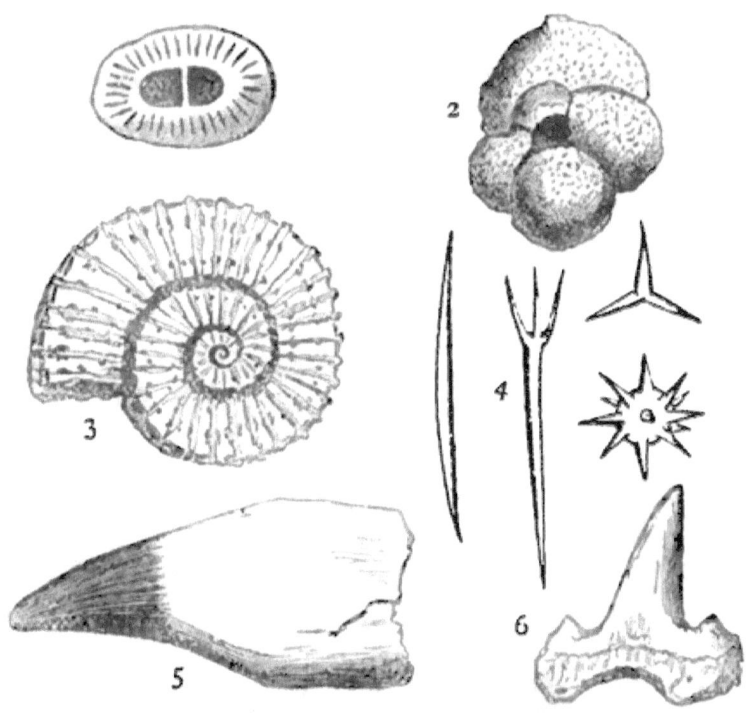

Various Fossils from the Cretaceous Formation.

1. *Coccolith* (much magnified) ; 2. *Globigerina*, a foraminifer (much magnified) ; 3. *Ammonites Rhotomagensis* ; 4. *Spicules* or Crystals of Fossil Sponges ; 5. Teeth of Marine Reptile (*Ichthyosaurus*) ; 6. Tooth of Shark (*Lamna*).

oceanic deposit. Its great thickness, the unaltered mineral character of the deposit of over so very extensive an area, as well as the peculiarity that it is mainly built up of broken or entire shells of *Foraminifera*, all point to this conclusion. No other kind of rock is better known than chalk. This chalk (when properly prepared) will yield to the microscopical investigator a large number of genera and species of oceanic *foraminifera*. One of the commonest of these chalk *foraminifera* is a species still abundant in the Pacific and Atlantic, along whose extended floors it and its congeners are forming a slimy ooze, just as chalk was originally elaborated. The name of this living foraminifer is *Globigerina bulloides*, and its equal abundance in the white chalk of England, in the *fossil* state, and in the blue oceanic waters of the Atlantic and Pacific, in the *living* condition, affords an additional evidence that the formation we are now speaking of was formed along the bottom of a deep and extensive sea.

To build up a dense, earthy, white rock like chalk to the thickness of more than a thousand feet (for the *Upper* Chalk alone is more than that in Norfolk), by the slow accumulation along the sea-floor of shells too small for the naked eye to perceive without assistance, must have occupied long periods of time. As they formed chalky ooze, the latter became the receptacle for such dead animals as found in it their last resting-place. The other and larger fossils of the Upper Chalk are just those we should expect to find in an oceanic deposit.

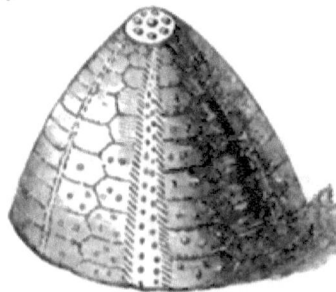

Fossil Sea-urchin (*Galerites albogalerus*).

THE WHITE CHALK OF ENGLAND. 205

They are nowhere abundant, and they are represented by species of Brachiopods (*Terebratula* and

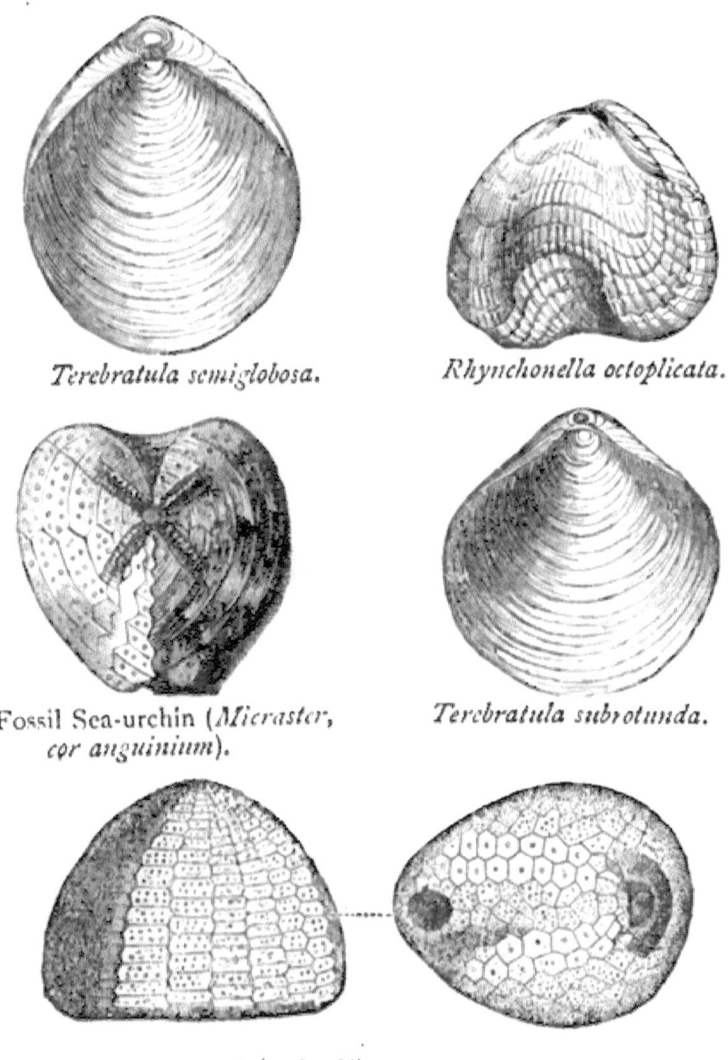

Terebratula semiglobosa.   *Rhynchonella octoplicata.*

Fossil Sea-urchin (*Micraster, cor anguinium*).   *Terebratula subrotunda.*

"Fairy-loaf" (*Ananchytes*).

Rhynchonella); small oysters of multiform shape and possessed of the power of so moulding themselves to the shape of any object which might happen to lie on the sea-bed as often to take a perfect cast of it; abundance of sea-urchins of all kinds; *Echini, Ananchytes, Galerites, Holaster, Micraster, Spatangus,* &c.; and remains of diminutive genera of sea-lilies. All of these deep-sea *Echinodermata* remind us of similar living species dredged up in the deeper parts of the Atlantic and Pacific during the recent "Challenger" expedition. Indeed, the naturalists on board proved that the abysmal parts of the sea still shelter some genera of echinoderms we had believed to be extinct,

Palatal Tooth of *Ptychodus polygyrus.*

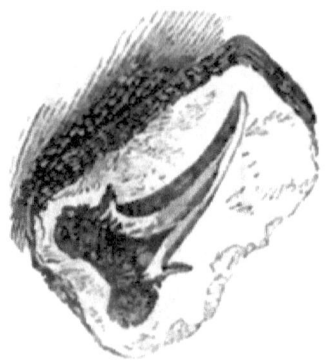

Tooth of *Lamna elegans.*

but which are found fossilized in the white chalk; as, for instance, *Salenia,* which is tolerably abundant in Norfolk, particularly in the flints.

In the white chalk we have more or less regular courses of flints, sometimes occurring as bands of fantastically-shaped nodules, and at other times (especially in the Lower Chalk) as thin, tabular plates. There is every reason for believing these flints to have been formed by organic agency, perhaps by the precipitation of silicates, induced by the decomposition of organic matter along the sea-floor, for it has been proved that such a process will bring about siliceous precipitation. This would cause the flint to assume a gelatinous condition, which would invest any shell, coral, or echinoderm, whose decomposing tissues had perhaps caused the chemical changes to be set in action. The mode in which the most delicate shells, sponges, sea-mats, &c., are imbedded in the now hard flints, sufficiently proves how soft and plastic the latter must have been when they were originally formed. In Norfolk we get huge flints imbedded one within another like a pile of basins in a crockery-shop, often to the height of 5 or 6 feet. They stand vertically to the strata, just as they were formed, and are believed to have been gigantic sponges, like "Neptune's cup." The name given to these fossils is *Paramoudra*.

All about London, and the eastern, south-eastern, and south-western counties, there are most extensive sheets of *flint gravel*. They often compose some of the Tertiary strata, such as the Bagshot sands. They likewise occur abundantly as post-glacial gravel throughout Suffolk and Norfolk. All these flints, rounded and angular, were originally formed organically at the bottom of the deep chalk sea, after the manner just indicated. All of them were originally imbedded in the white chalk. Hence we may infer to what extensive denudations the latter formation must have been subjected, even in England alone, from the quantity of flint-nodules and bands which have been liberated, broken up, rolled and gathered together to form these subsequently-deposited gravel-beds! The process undoubtedly went on throughout the entire Tertiary epoch, and there is every reason for believing that the white chalk once extended even into Scotland, for fragments of it have been found hermetically sealed up and preserved beneath the lavas which were ejected by the Mull volcano during the *Miocene* period.

But even in the chalk we occasionally get glimpses of the kind of life which existed out of the sea. Thus, we know that Flying Lizards (*Pterodactyles*), both tailed and tailless, abounded more than ever, and perhaps attained a greater size, some of them being as much as 20 feet across their outstretched wings! Marine reptiles (*Ichthyosauri*) were not so abundant in the sea, their places having been taken by another kind, which became extinct at the close of the Cretaceous era, called *Mososaurus*. The latter has been found in nearly a perfect state in the Upper Chalk near Norwich, where its teeth and bones are often met with. Its length was as much as 25 to 30 feet, and from the formidable character of its teeth we should say it was the tyrant of the seas. *Belemnites* (or "Thunderbolts," as they are popularly but erroneously called) are very plentiful in the chalk; next to them in abundance are *Ananchytes* (commonly called "Fairy Loaves") and bivalve shells, such as *Spondylus spinosus*.

We have evidence in the uppermost chalk strata elsewhere than England, that *true flowers* had at length appeared to adorn the world. As yet these were not of a highly-attractive kind. Associated with them the oak, maple, sycamore, and other true dicotyledonous trees and shrubs make their appearance. Thus, just at the close of the great secondary epoch we find preparations made as it were for its successor the Tertiary, which is noted for the abundance of its higher animal and vegetable life above all others. This may be largely due to the fact that during the whole Tertiary epoch the deposits were of a *local* character and no extensive oceanic strata then formed are known, inasmuch as the great oceanic areas were the same then as now, all the physical change having taken place on the sea-boards, or in shallow water.

CHAPTER XIV.

THE LATER LIFE OF THE WORLD.

THE Tertiary epoch is distinguished above its predecessors by the great influx of animal and vegetable forms of life allied to those still living. Few living *species* of animals have a geological antiquity as high as the commencement of this new era, although we have seen that one of the shelled animalcules (*Globigerina*) was as abundant and active during the Upper Cretaceous period as it is now. A species of brachiopod found fossilized in the Chalk (*Terebratula linearis*) is believed to be identical with a rare species

1   2

1. *Palæotherium magnum* (restored); a Tapir-like animal (Eocene Formation).
2. Skeleton of *Megatherium* (Miocene Formation).

still living in the deeper parts of the sea. These, however, are exceptions to the general rule.

But with the Tertiary epoch, at any rate, there commenced the existence of many genera of animals and plants which are still living somewhere in the world. In a few instances even the *species* have continued on to our time unaltered. And as we pass from the commencement of the Tertiary age and approach our own we are particularly struck by the increasing resemblances which the fossils bear to living forms of life, until at length we see them merging into each other, and fossil forms and existing types blend together. It is this gradually-increasing relationship between the extinct and living types that has caused geologists to separate the Tertiary epoch into its four great stages or periods, according to the percentages of living species which have been found among the fossils of each subdivision.

The *Eocene* period ("Dawn of Recent" life) found Europe (including Great Britain) enjoying a climate different from that which now characterizes these latitudes. It was almost *tropical* in its temperature, and consequently the life of the period in many respects resembled that of some countries under the equator. In the sea, in the rivers, on the dry land, although *Eocene* animals are nearly all extinct, we cannot but recognise their tropical appearance. This will be more evident as we proceed.

The *Eocene* formation is well represented in Great Britain, although in that "patchy" form which distinguishes the Tertiary strata when compared with the extensive spread of the Primary systems of rocks. On the Continent and in America there is similar evidence of Tertiary strata being deposited in lake-basins, estuaries, &c., although perhaps the largest and finest development of the early Tertiary rocks is to be found in some of the western States of North America, notably in Kansas, Wyoming, Dakotah, and elsewhere. In these latter places the strata are often thousands of feet in thickness, full of animal and plant-remains much more complete in their history of the life of the period perhaps than is afforded elsewhere on the globe. The geological history of this district is being worked out by the United States Geological Surveyor in the completest manner, and when it is fully presented to the world it will read like a fairy tale.

The student will find in all good works on geology the various details respecting the subdivisions of the Eocene strata, into which it is not necessary for us here to enter. The lower are called "Thanet," "Woolwich," "Reading," and "Oldhaven" beds. At the various places whose names are here mentioned the reader will find sections showing each stratum.

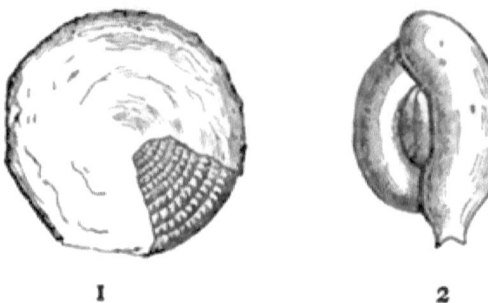

Characteristic *Foraminifera* from the Eocene Marine Strata.
1. *Nummulites;* 2. *Miliola.* (Both magnified.)

In the Isle of Thanet, where we find the lowest beds, the latter are of a yellowish-green or buff colour, and the fossils are usually in the shape of impressions or "casts" only; although there are places where we find such genera of fossil shells as *Corbula, Cyprina,*

&c., well preserved. The best localities for observing this stratum are at Herne Bay, the cliffs of Pegwell Bay, the sand-pits at Charlton, near Woolwich, and others on the south side of London. Mr. Whitaker has noticed them at Sudbury, in Suffolk, and they are also to be seen near Ipswich. The "Woolwich and Reading beds" are most thickly developed in Whitecliff Bay. They are also seen in the cliffs of Alum Bay, as well as at the places whose names they bear. The characters of this bed change very much; sometimes it is sandy, at others full of green-coated angular flints. At others it is bright-coloured, mottled, "plastic clay," as in Berkshire, North Hampshire, and part of Surrey; or it is a thick, compact bed of oyster-shells, as at Bromley. Great quantities and a considerable variety of fossils have been found in this bed, nearly all of them being of marine habits. Perhaps the most notable are the remains of an extinct animal nearly allied to the Tapir, called *Coryphodon*. Fossil turtles occur in the same rock. The "Oldhaven beds" are chiefly composed of rolled flint pebbles, usually imbedded in sand, and occasionally cemented thereby into a kind of pudding-stone. They are to be seen in the neighbourhood of Canterbury, Rochester, on Plumstead Common, at Blackheath, Woolwich, and elsewhere. The fossils are both of a marine and estuarine character, indicating that all the beds were formed near the old shores, and that fresh water debouched into the sea.

But the most important of all the Eocene strata is that called the "London Clay." It is perhaps the most extensive of all the Tertiary beds, and formerly it undoubtedly covered a larger area than it does now, for there is evidence of a great thickness having been removed by denudation, especially in Norfolk. It crops out in the cliffs of the Suffolk and Essex coasts, extends under the Metropolis (whence its name), continues to Hampshire, and the Isle of Wight. Its thickness is about 500 feet, and from its fossils (which are very numerous in some places, and nearly absent in others) there can be no question that it is a purely marine deposit. Professor Rupert Jones, judging by the fossil foraminifera yielded by the London Clay, concludes it was deposited in about one hundred fathom water. Some parts could not have been formed far from land, however, as there are imbedded the remains of land animals and reptiles, plants, trees, &c., all of which were evidently carried to the sea by the rivers.

But no matter how we look at the fossils of this interesting deposit, we are assured of the higher temperature which then prevailed. The marine shells belong to genera whose names at once call up to the mind of the conchologist West Indian and other tropical forms. Such are *Pleurotoma*, *Rostellaria*, *Voluta*, *Nautilus* (of several species), and many others. The Sea-urchins equally indicate warm seas. The Fossil Fish are allied to the White Shark (only much larger), the Saw-fish, the Sword-fish, &c. *Palæophis* is a species of Sea-serpent at least 13 feet in length, which lived in the London Clay sea. Many kinds of marine turtles abounded, and their perfect carapaces are often found in the "cement-stones" which take the place in the London

Clay that flint-nodules do in the chalk. Remains of true *Crocodiles* have been dug out in several localities.

But the Fossil Flora is unquestionably the most important in its bearings upon the climature of this period. We know that the dry land must have been clothed with a vegetation analogous to that which now luxuriates in the Malayan Archipelago. In the Isle of Sheppey (one of the most notable fossiliferous localities of the London Clay) we actually find *banks* of fossil palm-fruits called *Nipadites*, allied to those which still so accumulate on the surface of the river Ganges as to impede the steam navigation and clog the paddles of the river boats. More than a dozen species of these palm-fruits have been described. Sheppey has also yielded more than one hundred species of fossil plants, nearly all of which are related to genera still living in much warmer latitudes; such as custard-apples, gourds, &c. *Palæotheria*, or tapir-like animals, abounded on the dry land ; and recently a fossil bird has been found (*Odontopteryx*), whose mandibles were provided with bony teeth ! Opossums swarmed in the forests of this period, and at its close *Monkeys* seem to have made their first appearance on the globe. *Ganoid* fish still lived in the rivers, and their remains have been found at Kyson, near Woodbridge, in Suffolk, associated with those of large bats, water-snakes, &c. These ancient forests were the haunts of *Pythons*, *Hyænodons* (a creature with the joint character of a tiger and a hyæna), and other predatory animals.

The middle Eocene beds succeed the London Clay, comprising the Bagshot sands and gravels.

Bracklesham beds, Barton Clay, &c. Here and there we get plenty of fossil plants, as in the famous "leaf

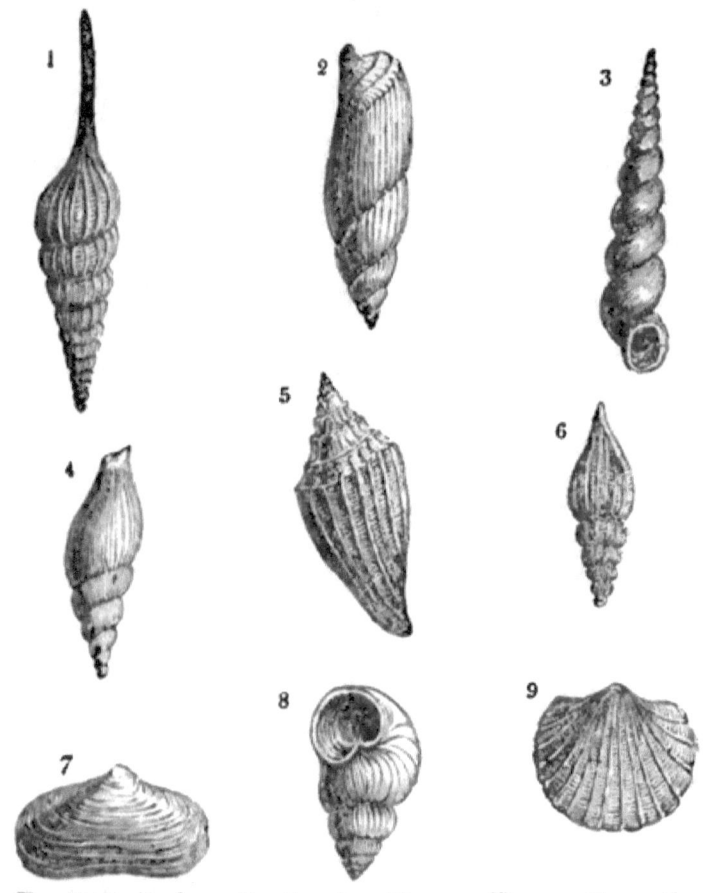

Fossil Shells from the London Clay, or Eocene Formation.
1. *Fusus asper.*
2. *Ancillaria subulata.*
3. *Turritella imbricataria.*
4. *Limnæa longiscata.*
5. *Voluta lucatrix.*
6. *Rostellaria rimosa.*
7. *Sanguinolaria compressa.*
8. *Paludina lenta.*
9. *Pectunculus scalaris.*

beds" of Bournemouth and Alum Bay. From these we infer that the climature was of a more pronounced tropical character during the middle of the Eocene period than it was at the beginning or the end. At Bournemouth the most beautiful impressions of the leaves, fruits, &c., of tropical palms and other plants have been found, all of them pointing to humidity and warmth of climate. The fossil flora of Alum Bay is remarkable for its number of species allied to the *Acacias*. Acacias, figs, dryandras, fan-palms, &c., appear to have been the most numerous. The remarkable fact about our English Eocene flora is its resemblance to that of tropical Australia. The abundance of *Proteaceous* plants (now characteristic of the Australian region) is that which renders the similitude most complete.

The Bracklesham beds are exceedingly fossiliferous in places. Although they take their name from the place in Sussex, it is these beds of white, yellow, and crimson sand, and *lignite* seams, which give to the cliffs of Alum Bay their well-known attractiveness. The Lignite seams (like the coal seams in the South Wales coal-field) always rest on stiff beds of clay. The Barton Clay is remarkable for its beautiful and well-preserved fossil shells, the very look of which suggests recent tropical or warm temperate species. At Hordwell and Barton cliffs these beds are about 300 feet thick, and often full of the most lovely fossils, such as *Rostellaria*, *Voluta*, *Typhis*, and large foraminifera, called *Nummulites*.

The Upper Eocene is almost wholly represented in England by strata called "fluvio-marine," from its associated fresh-water, brackish, and marine fossils. In the Isle of Wight, at Headon, Osborne, Bembridge, and Hempstead, these beds are well developed. Sometimes entire hills are seen to be composed of fresh-water or marine shells. Here and there remains of crocodiles, turtles, &c., have been met with. This upper series of Eocene beds is about 500 feet in thickness. Similar strata are found in the Vienna and Paris basins, and the limestones used in the erection of the palatial houses in those great cities are seen to be composed by the agglomeration of minute shells which lived about this stage of the Tertiary epoch.

The Middle Period, called *Miocene*, is little represented in British geology, although we know it was a remarkable epoch in the history of the northern hemisphere. From the extraordinary development of the strata in Arctic regions, cropping out from under the ice and snow sheets, some important inferences may be drawn. In Greenland, Spitzbergen, and as high as eighty-two degrees north latitude, Miocene strata have been found, containing seams of lignite and abundance of fossil plants. Some of the latter are even southerly types; none of them could now exist where they are now found fossilized. And even if they could find warmth enough, we should have to strip off the ice and snow which now swathe those regions. It is evident, therefore, that during the *Miocene* period no ice-cap existed at the North Pole to extend down to the Arctic Circle, and the probability is that forests existed beneath the very pole-star!

Everywhere the flora of the Miocene formation speaks distinctly of a very warm climature, although not a tropical one, as existing about this time. This is the opinion of Professor Heer, who has devoted his life to the study of the fossil plants and insects found in the strata of this particular age. He holds that the combined evidence of the fossil flora points to a climate which was on an average sixteen degrees higher than it is now over the same latitudes.

Flowers had by this time multiplied upon the face of the earth, and many gaily-blossomed species expanded their corollas in the warm sunshine. Butterflies, bees, wasps, ants, and even the *white* ants (*termites*) abounded in places. The northern hemisphere was now clad in a dense robe of vegetation. We get a glimpse of the richness and variety of the flora which adorned the world at this time from the fossil plants exhumed from that wonderful storehouse at Oenigen, in Switzerland. The beds containing them were originally quietly deposited along the bottom of an extensive fresh-water lake, and it is literally surprising how perfectly leaves, flowers, and fruit have been preserved. Every vein is still shown on the leaves, by means of which we can make out even the species of some of them. No fewer than eight hundred species of *flower-bearing* plants have been described from these beds alone, and about two thousand species altogether, including the non-flowering species, such as ferns, mosses, lichens, diatoms, &c. Several hundred species of fossil Miocene plants have come from Iceland and Greenland, others from Spitzbergen, the Alaska Islands, Kamtschatka, and Japan. Singularly enough the flora, as a whole, whilst still possessing Australian kinds, includes many which are now abundant in the Southern States of North America, such as magnolias, tulip-trees, wellingtonias, &c. The commonest of European plants at this time were smilax, camphor-trees, dryandras, fig-trees, palm-trees, banksias, sequoias, gardenias, vines, and laurels.

In France there were large lakes in the centre of that country, where limestone beds were formed. The country supported enormous quantities of wild animals of curious extinct types, such as *anoplotheria*, *palæotheria*, tapirs, river-hogs, pigs, deer without antlers, antelopes, elks, *acerotheria*, &c., on which preyed *hyænodon*, *anthracotherium*, &c. The carcases of these animals strewed the plains, and their bones were afterwards dissolved by the agency of the weather and carried by the water into the cracks, fissures, and caverns which extend into the Oolitic limestones beneath, where the matter has accumulated in stalagmitic masses of phosphate of lime. It is in these "phosphorite deposits," as they are called, in the south of France, that we get a perfect museum of early Miocene animals, among which we have just named the most abundant, although there is proof of monkeys, lemurs, crocodiles, and huge serpents and vampire bats having lived thereabouts during the same period.

In England, perhaps, the only place where undoubtedly Miocene strata occur are the Lignite, or *brown coal* beds of Bovey Tracy in Devonshire. These are about 200 or 300 feet in thickness, and the remains of about fifty species of Miocene plants have been obtained from them; among which the chief are wellingtonias (or *sequoias*), evergreen oaks, figs, prickly palms, cinnamon-trees, ferns, &c. In the island of Mull the Duke of Argyll has described certain Miocene plant-beds, which were subsequently covered up by a stream of molten lava that issued from the Mull volcanoes. One species of fern has been found in these beds which has not been met with elsewhere.

The *Miocene* period is more remarkable in British geology for its *igneous* rather than its sedimentary deposits. This was, as we have before remarked, the period when volcanic activity was felt for the last time in the British islands. At least five or six active volcanoes were then in existence in the isles of Mull, Ram, Eiff, Antrim, and near Edinburgh. In central France a very large number (more than one hundred) of volcanoes were in operation, and these now form the conical hill-scenery about Clermont, which have also amalgamated together the old weathered rocks of the central mountains by their flows of trachytic lava. Mounts Etna and Vesuvius as yet were not volcanoes; the Alps were nothing like the extensive and high mountain-chain they now are; lacustrine deposits of enormous thickness were then forming at the base of the much lower Himalayan Mountains; whilst the Andes may have been some thousands of feet lower than they are now. Nearly all Great Britain was a dry land surface, peopled with tapirs, three-toed horses (*Hipparion*), pigs, mastodons (an extinct kind of elephant), rhinoceri, deer, leopards, &c., whose bones and teeth were left strewn upon the bare ground; and so when the latter became depressed to form a shallow sea-floor (as it did early in the subsequent period), these teeth and bones were covered over by, and lay at the bottom of, the next marine deposits, which are the well-known "Crag" beds of Norfolk and Suffolk.

CHAPTER XV.

THE "GREAT ICE AGE."

WE have seen the evidence afforded by the fossil plants of the *Eocene* and *Miocene* periods as to the higher temperature of the climate which then marked the northern hemisphere. Further, we had incidentally to notice that it was much higher during mid-Eocene time than in the Miocene. Now we come to speak of the *Pliocene* period, and we shall find in its earlier-formed strata still further evidence of the decrease of warmth, and in the later beds actually of the first indications of the setting-in of *cold* conditions; and in the *Pleistocene* period this cold, we shall find, has so increased that *Arctic*, instead of *tropical* climature characterized those areas of the Northern Hemisphere occupied by the British islands! Thus we have sure geological evidence, not to be gainsaid, of the pendulum-like swinging of the climature from a sub-tropical state in the *Eocene* to *Arctic* cold in the *Pleistocene* period! The latter is on this account also called the "Great Ice Age," the "Glacial Period," &c., all of which betoken the geological evidence its beds afford of the climature under which they were formed.

Let us speak of the *Pliocene* era first. It is represented in the eastern counties of England by thick beds of fossil shells, called "crag," at the bottom of which lie undoubted remains of Miocene animals (as mentioned in the last chapter), commingled with those of a still older period, the Eocene, for the London Clay has had large quantities of its own fossils worn out of it by the action of the weather during the long period that England was dry land. Accordingly we find London Clay fossils (usually changed into phosphate), as crabs, fish, turtles, shark's teeth, wood, &c., mixed up with the bones of Miocene land animals, and the characteristic shells of the Crag. Some of these London Clay fossils have been bored into by the boring mollusca of the Pliocene seas, and in a few instances the shells are still in the chambers thus excavated!

These "Crag" beds are especially interesting to the young geological student; they abound with a variety of fossils, and these can be easily obtained. In some of the pits you see a section of 20 or 30 feet made up entirely of loose shells, corals, fish-teeth, &c., any of which you can take out with the finger and thumb! The "coprolites" (as the phosphatic nodules and fossils are called, most of which have been weathered out of the London Clay) have been much sought after in Suffolk. They are ground to powder, and, when properly prepared, converted into rich phosphatic manures of high fertilizing power. Thus has man learned the practical art of converting stones into bread! More than one million pounds' worth of these precious little phosphate stones have been raised from the base of the "Red crag" since their utility was first made known by Professor Henslow some thirty years ago.

The Pliocene period in Britain is represented by three beds, called the "Coralline," "Red," and "Norwich Crags," whose relative ages to each other stand in the order their names are here placed. In the Coralline Crag, which is found only in a few places in Suffolk, being best developed about Orford, we find there about three hundred and fifty species of fossil shells which have been figured and described, besides one hundred and thirty species of sea-mats (some of them, as *Fascicularia*, of peculiar structure) and numbers of fossil lamp-shells, sea-urchins, fish, corals, foraminifera, &c. Peculiar bottle-nosed whales (*Choneziphius* and *Belemnoziphius*) were then tolerably abundant, and their snouts are found fossilized.

The molluscan fauna of the Coralline Crag, however, shows us that warmth-loving species still lived in British latitudes, such as *Voluta, Pyrula, Conus, Cassidaria*, &c. At the same time it should be stated that among the fossil shells we have an overpowering abundance of the genus *Astarte*, always a cold-loving kind. So that the sea of the Coralline Crag would appear to have been affected by extremes of climature; and this is substantiated by the presence of large boulders of quartz, pudding-stone, oolitic limestone, and flints (many of them completely covered by fossil barnacles) which abound at the base of the Red Crags. In short, there are about twenty-eight species of mollusca which we might call *Southern*, on account of their being now found in seas more to the south. For it should be remembered that we now find numerous species of shells of exactly the same kind as those still living somewhere or another in these Crag beds; and so the inferences as to climate become safer.

In the succeeding Red Crag there have been found about two hundred and fifty species of fossil shells, besides sea-urchins, &c. Sea-mats were not now so abundant. Among this list of shells we only find *thirteen* species which are "Southern," whilst the "Northern" species have considerably increased; and thus we get double evidence of the gradual refrigeration of the climate. The third, or *Norwich Crag*, appears to have been an estuarine deposit, of the same age or a little later, as that when the Red Crag was formed. In the Norwich Crag, however, we find *no* "Southern" species of mollusca at all, whilst there appear actually *Arctic* species, in nearly Arctic proportions; and in a higher bed (Chillesford Crag) formed at a still later date, the abundance of Arctic mollusca is perfectly astonishing.

Nothing could be completer than the climatal changes thus indicated even by our English Pliocene fossils, which are supplemented by physical and other evidence; to say nothing of the inferences so plainly pointed out by the study of preceding and succeeding geological formations. In Sicily, about the latter part of the time our Crag beds were being slowly formed, and for a long time afterwards, a great limestone formation was elaborated. It is full of fossils, and among them are certain species of shells which are absent in the Great Britain strata, but which existed in our seas whilst the Crag was formed. As the cold increased, these species emigrated to the south, and took up their places in the Mediterranean, where they abounded: nearly half the entire island of Sicily is covered with Pliocene deposits, to the thickness of 2,000 feet. Mount Etna had not then commenced its existence. All the mass of volcanic material which now builds it up to the height of 11,000 feet, has accumulated around the vent since the close of the Pliocene period. In Italy, near Florence, there was an extensive lake, along whose floor nearly 1,000 feet of strata were formed.

Near Cromer there are very high cliffs, and at low water there may be seen cropping out from beneath them and extending seaward so as to form its bed, an ancient forest. The tree-trunks still extend into the ancient soils, and the latter are interstratified with fresh-water deposits, showing there was a lake once where the German Ocean rolls now. From the strata of this "forest bed" (as it is called) there have been exhumed the remains of yew-trees, spruce pine, Scotch fir, oak, alder, birch, beside ferns, water-lilies, &c. The land animals are represented by remains of rhinoceros, hippopotamus, elephant (three species), bear, beaver, &c. This "forest bed" is believed to be about the same age (or a little later) as the Norwich crag. Anyhow it is *Preglacial*, that is to say, it existed before the extreme Arctic climature set so rigorously in, for we can see the boulder clays of the cliffs resting upon it.

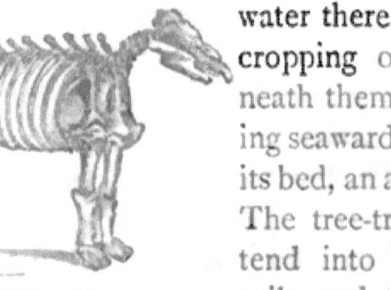
Skeleton of the *Mastodon*.

The Glacial period was the last of the great geological eras. It must have extended over a very long

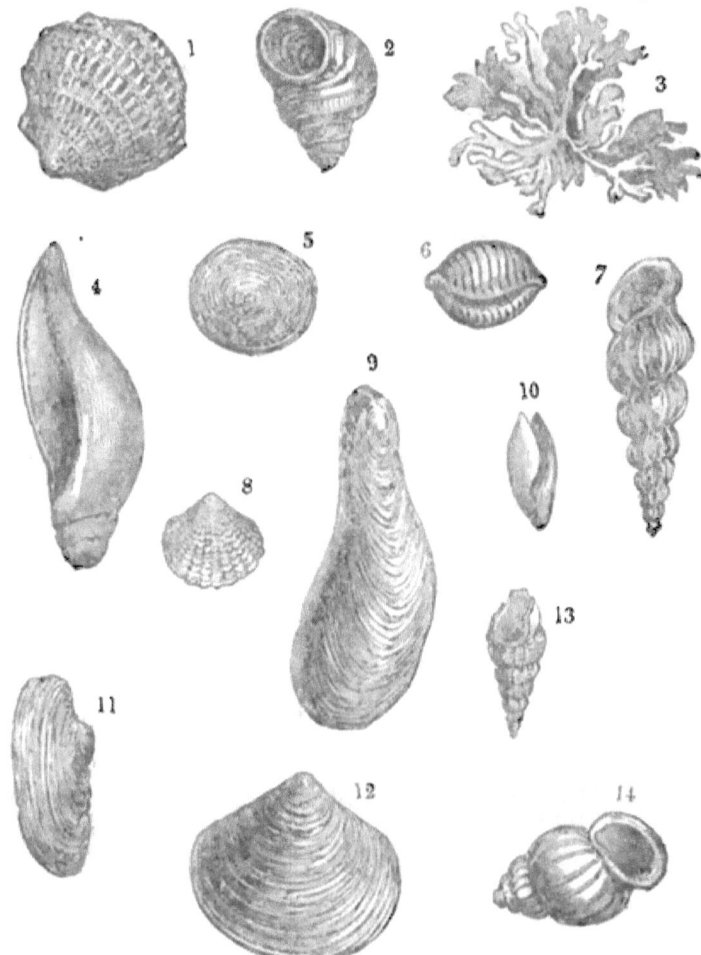

Fossils from the "Crags" (Newer Tertiary), or Pliocene Formation.

1. *Fascicularia aurantium.*
2. *Littorina littorea.*
3. *Tubulipora.*
4. *Voluta Lamberti.*
5. *Patella æqualis.*
6. *Cypræa avellana.*
7. *Scalaria similis.*
8. *Cardita scalaris.*
9. *Modiola.*
10. *Bulla cylindracea.*
11. *Saxicava rugosa.*
12. *Tellina crassa.*
13. *Nassa elegans.*
14. *Paludina unicolor.*

time, and we have proof that the rigour of the climate was more than once assuaged before the period came to a close. The deposits which were then formed are represented by the "boulder clays," which cover so large an area of northern, midland and eastern England, as well as the beds of sand and gravel with which these *boulder clays* are so frequently interstratified. To account for the contrastable and extreme changes of climate which the fossils of the *Eocene* and *Pleistocene* or Glacial period so plainly indicate, some have thought it necessary to assume that the pole of the earth has shifted, or that the earth's crust has somehow slipped over its internal molten nucleus, so as to bring different areas of the surface alternately under the influence of tropical heat or Arctic cold. But if the reader will turn to Dr. James Croll's "Climate and Time," he will there find facts enough to show how no such extreme hypothesis is needed, and that there are certain actual astronomical changes to which our earth is subject, which set up physical influences powerful enough to bring about all the changes in climate which geology testifies have really taken place.

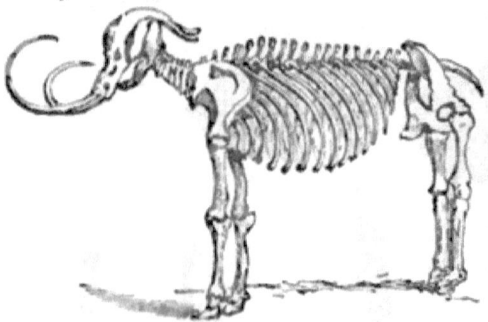

Skeleton of Mammoth, or *Elephas Primigenius*.

Skeleton of Irish Elk (*Megaceros*).

The *Pleistocene* or Glacial period appears to have been characterised, in Great Britain at least, by three remarkable series of geological operations. During the era when the first set were at work a considerable elevation of this country took place, and this was attended by an extreme Arctic climature. Afterwards, in the second era, we have evidence of a great depression or subsidence, when the lower part of the country was covered by a wintry sea, in which icebergs abounded. During the third stage an elevation of Great Britain once more took place, and the climate showed signs of modification, although glaciers still filled the mountain valleys. It is evident that these great changes could not have been effected in a short space of time, and there is not the slightest reason to think they were otherwise than slow in their operation. During the first era the hills and mountains of Wales, Cumberland, North Lancashire and Yorkshire, Scotland and Ireland, stood relatively higher above the sea-level than they do now. All the high land was swathed in an extended ice-sheet, as Greenland is at the present time. This ice-sheet was in slow movement seawards, as we know is usually the case with "continental" ice, and its mechanical power upon the underlying rocks was so great as to crush and grind them into mud. In this way was formed the "till" or boulder-clay of the northern counties and Scotland. Sometimes very large boulders are seen imbedded in it, weighing many tons each. These are always formed of rocks which naturally occur further to the north, and they must have been conveyed to where we find them by some such carrying agency as that of ice. However, all the boulders which are hard enough to retain them, little and big, bear marks of ice-action in scratches, polishing, etc., exactly resembling those you may see at any time in the heaps of rubbish brought down by the Swiss glaciers. The sides of the hills and mountains, and even the highest peaks of all our high lands, are still scratched where the ice-sheet moved over their surfaces. We always find *lakes* to be accompaniments of mountain scenery, and many of our best geologists are of opinion that these are simply "rock basins," scooped out by the agency of moving ice where its mechanical power was greatest. Hence, now that the ice has all been melted off the surface these rock-basins are filled with water. At Windermere, Ullswater, Coniston, and elsewhere in the lake district of England, you may see large moraine heaps around the margins, and rounded bosses of rock dotting their surfaces as islands. These are all of them certain marks of ice-action. The same phenomena occur in North Wales and Scotland in even a more marked degree.

This era of elevation was followed by one of *subsidence*, and we are not without means of judging to what extent the depression took place. Near Carnarvon is a high hill called Moel Tryfaen, and near its summit, at a height of about 1,600 feet, is actually a "raised beach," from which about thirty species of recent shells, mostly of Arctic kinds, have been obtained. This ancient beach, therefore, marks the depth to which the submergence must have taken place, for we cannot suppose one hill to be shifted from its place and submerged by itself.

Moreover, there are other hills in North Wales and elsewhere which tell a similar tale. It was most probably at this stage that the midland and eastern counties were strewn with the ice-derived rubbish called boulder clay. The wolds of Yorkshire suffered dreadfully, for we find in the eastern counties the upper boulder clay is crammed full of chalk rubbish and oolitic boulders; and in the Cromer cliffs you may see enormous masses of chalk, 200 feet each in length, and 30 or 40 feet thick, which have been brought by icebergs to their present sites. You can plainly see now where they were dropped on the muddy sea-bed; they squeezed the ooze out, for all round these huge chalk boulders the crags and clays are contorted and twisted in the most remarkable manner. This wintry sea endured long enough to strew the greater part of England with the rich subsoils of sand, gravel, and clay, which now play so important a part in our agricultural prosperity.

When the third stage of this period set in there was a reversal of the physical conditions of land and sea. Upheaval had once more set in, the wintry sea gradually disappeared, until at length England was joined to the rest of Europe as a continued westerly extension. Similarly, Ireland was a land connection of England, by way of what is now the Isle of Man. The climate gradually became milder, the ice-sheet slowly disappeared; but for a long time afterwards glaciers still filled the larger mountain valleys, where they ploughed out the rubbish that had accumulated previously, and which had not been re-arranged (as was the case in Scotland and Ireland during the submergence era) into those long, low lines of *straths*, *dunes*, and *eskers*, which so plainly diversify the landscape scenery of central Ireland and the plains of Scotland. The course of some of the ancient glaciers can still be seen. Their *moraines* are abundant in all our hilly and mountainous districts. Even the distribution of the Arctic plants on the slopes and tops of our hilly ranges, and of the northern mollusca met with in the deeper and colder parts of the sea around our coasts, is only to be explained by reference to the overwhelming cold of the Glacial period. The woolly-haired mammoth (*Elephas primigenius*) and woolly-haired rhinoceros, both of them then specially adapted to survive the rigours of a cold climate, abounded in England, and their teeth and tusks and bones are often met with in deposits which were then formed. The fossil-shells imbedded during the submergence stage belong mostly to Arctic species; although during the warmer intervals of climate to which we have already alluded other species of mollusca abounded better suited to the change than the Arctic and cold-loving kinds.

Thus we see that the irregular beds of boulder clay, sand, gravel heaps, and detached boulders, of North Wales, Lancashire, Yorkshire, Cumberland, or Scotland, have a story of their own, which completes the geological narrative of the extensive physical changes to which our planet has been subjected since it first left the hands of its Creator! Everywhere, even amidst what appears to be chaos and confusion, there are thus evolved *law* and *order;* which latter, the poet tells us, is "Heaven's first law!"

CHAPTER XVI.

FOSSILIFEROUS LOCALITIES.

THERE is a popular saying which declares that "seeing is believing." The youthful reader, whose mind is struck for the first time with the romantic revelations of geology respecting the antiquity of our globe, and the animals and plants which formerly inhabited it, but are now extinct and buried in the rocks beneath our feet, is even more affected when he is taken for the first time to some rock in which he can see the fossils imbedded. Here is such ocular demonstration as he never expected, and the "hunting instinct," which is more or less strong in all of us, comes out as he begins to disinter the petrified organic remains.

The common idea of most geological students is that fossiliferous localities are at a distance from their own homes. They have never seen any of the fossils they read or hear about, and so at once conclude there cannot be any in their own districts. But the eye brings with it the power of seeing, and it is not long after a student knows what fossils are, and under what conditions they occur, that he begins to find them. Then a new and almost poetic halo is thrown around objects formerly deemed the most commonplace. Pebbles are no longer accidental things, but fragments of old rocks, broken off and rolled by the waves of forgotten sea-shores. A piece of coal is not what it is to the vulgar eye—something to burn, and which costs so much a ton: it is a fragment of a mineralized forest which was once waved by primeval gales and breezes, and stimulated into growth by the light and heat of the sun ages ago.

There are few sciences which are more dependent on others than that of geology. Certainly there is none which sends the young student so eagerly to other sciences for assistance. The fossils he meets with in the rocks are far more abundant than he imagined before he began to study geology. Indeed, one of the chief causes of wonder to the young geologist, when his eyes are thoroughly opened, is the abundance of fossil remains within the immediate neighbourhood of his home, unless the latter happen to be on the old granite or metamorphic rocks. He wonders how it is he never noticed them before. Fragments or whole specimens of fossils, animal and vegetable, are constantly turning up before his eager and enthusiastic eyes, either in the parent rocks or in the boulder clays and drifts which have been formed out of them. The very rocks of the hills and mountains seem to be almost wholly composed of them; nay, the solid dry land of the globe appears to have been mainly put together by the agency or through the instrumentality of Life! The abodes of all living forms are on the sepulchres of the dead! Existence and extinction are strangely associated together.

No sooner has the young beginner appreciated the wealth of objects by which he is surrounded, or to which he may obtain easy access, than the first fit of *collecting* takes possession of him. His holidays are spent in fossiliferous localities; and his leisure time in reading about them, or in arranging his cabinet. At length he feels the need for more knowledge than he possesses about the many strange forms he comes across. He has an idea they are something altogether different from anything now existing, and a feeling of something like *disappointment* comes over him when he learns that they are constructed on the same plan, and that in many instances the same generic and even specific forms are still in existence. This state of mind, however, soon gives way to thorough admiration, for he now catches a glimpse of the life-plan of the globe. He sees that, beginning with the lowest and humblest of organisms, it has graduated into the present fauna and flora; that the stream of life, issuing like a rill from such obscure springs as are hardly descernible in the distant Laurentian period, has been gaining in volume and depth as it has passed onward, in unbroken continuity, through all the succeeding ages, until it has opened out in the grand ocean of existing life! Every fossil he picks up is a letter in the great stone book, and many such letters, properly put together, have spelled out some of the most wonderful generalizations that have come before the human mind. For geology as a science is peculiar in this respect, that in proportion to the degree of intellectual labour bestowed upon it, the resulting knowledge is wider and broader than that afforded by any other science, except, perhaps, astronomy.

Geology is essentially an open-air study. It leads a man into the most beautiful of landscapes, to the most charming of scenery. The tame flatness of the plains reveals to him comparatively little, unless coal or salt mining has partly turned the earth's crust inside out, or railway-cuttings have laid open sections instructive both as regards the strata and the fossils they contain. Boulder-clay pits or natural tarns will even here occasionally prove interesting. But to study the stony science in its fulness we must " gang to the hills !" There, where the heather is purplest, and the atmosphere exhilarates like old wine, you are most likely to read off the "record of the rocks!" Healthful activity is necessarily gendered; and the memory is stored with remembrances of sunny days and clear skies, never to be forgotten!

The so-called British Laurentian rocks have as yet yielded no fossils, but the Cambrian formation, once deemed so poverty-stricken in organic remains, has lately yielded up abundance of fossils under more extended and diligent observation. The richest of these fossiliferous localities are in the neighbourhood of St. David's, where organic remains have been discovered in abundance by Dr. Hicks. These fossils include representatives of many different groups of animal life, as sponges, annelids (or worms), crustaceans (as Trilobites, Entomostraca, &c.), Brachiopods, and true mollusca. Among others we get the huge Trilobite *Paradoxides Davidis*, nearly two feet in length. The name *Menevian* is given to these strata, from the ancient Roman name of St. David's. They form the upper part of the Lower Cambrian rocks. The Lingula Flags occur in the Middle Cambrian, and, as their name imports, they are usually rich in the fossils which give to them their name, particularly in the neighbourhood of Tremadoc, in North Wales. Cambrian fossils may also be found in certain bands of softer slates than usual about Dolgelly, Portmadoc, Harlech, Festiniog; in the rocks of Ragged-stone Hill, overlooking the Hollybush Valley, in the Malverns; in the black shale overlying this Hollybush sandstone along the Malverns, where is abundance and variety of Trilobites. The rocks of the Arenig mountains, in Merionethshire, are in places crowded with fossils belonging to nearly every kind of invertebrate animal. Many of these fossil remains are but feebly preserved, and frequently all the evidence of their existence is in the shape of impressions or "casts." In Cumberland we have strata of the same age as the Upper Cambrian rocks of North Wales, and in various localities, as at Dufton, Swindale, Pusgill, &c., fossils are found. The Bala limestone is in places full of fossils, but perhaps the best locality for them in all North Wales is at Mynydd Fronfrys, near Llangollen, where the young geologist may soon fill his bag with a rich and varied assortment, and meantime get one of the finest views in Britain as well. At Hirnant, near Bala, we have another good locality for fossils; and the ardent student may find them abundantly, as casts, on the top of Snowdon.

Near Carnarvon, about two miles out of the town, on the road to Bedgellert, the rambler comes to where the river Seiont crosses the high road, and he may observe that the escarpment forming the further bank of the river is formed of black shales. These are rich in various species of *Graptolites*. But perhaps the best hunting-ground for these beautiful fossils is in a pretty tree-shadowed gorge cut by a moutain-stream, which may be found by directly ascending the hill behind Low Wood Hotel, near Windermere. The black slates which crop out on each side the ravine and form the floor over which the stream purls, are full of very pretty *Graptolites*, converted into iron sulphite (iron pyrites), so that they look as if the slates were gilded with them. At Moffat, in Dumfries-shire, we have similar black shales (the Graptolites are seldom or never found except in *black* shales), in places actually crowded with these interesting objects.

On the hillsides above Troutbeck, near Windermere, the Coniston limestone may be easily found, for it rises higher than the rest of the rocks, being harder. It is one mass of casts and impressions of all kinds of invertebrate fossils, particularly corals and brachiopods.

The Silurian rocks have recently been separated from the Cambrian at a different horizon than formerly; so that many strata not long ago called Lower Silurian, are now included among the Upper Cambrian beds. But even under the new classification, the Silurian strata proper are often very full of fossils. About Wrexham, Builth, and Llandovery, the Lower Silurian strata are very rich in that peculiar fossil brachiopod called *Pentamerus*, and the student will find it in most outcrops of the Lower

Llandovery beds. Higher up in the series we have a stratum so crowded with this fossil that it goes by their name. At May Hill we may find abundance of all kinds of invertebrate organisms. The Wenlock beds (so called from the typical development of these strata in Shropshire) are frequently very fossiliferous, and especially at the place whence they derive their name. Near Conway, Plas Madoc, Pentre Voilas, and notably at the flag and slate quarries about three miles from Llangollen, any number of characteristic fossils may be found. At the last-mentioned locality the fossil Encrinites are often preserved entire—heads, arms, pelvis, and stems. Woolhope, near Hereford, is another celebrated fossil-hunting place, the organic remains being very perfectly preserved, and not difficult of extraction. The Wenlock limestone occurs at the place which gives to this stratum its name, and this bed is perhaps the most remarkable of any of the Silurian strata for its abundance and variety of fossils. Wenlock Edge, in Shropshire, is full of fossil corals. The same rock forms the Wren's nest at Dudley, and is there so full of all kinds of marine fossils, that one can hardly put the tip of one's finger on an unoccupied place.

At Ludlow, near the castle, is the celebrated "Fish-bone bed," a few inches in thickness, but full of the small teeth, scales, &c., of small fossil fishes (chiefly *Onchus*)—almost the first to appear in the seas of the globe. The "bone-bed" extends for a distance of nearly forty miles. At Leintwardine, where the flag-stone quarries occur, the student may purchase fossil star-fish, some of them exceedingly perfect, from the workmen.

The localities where Devonian fossils are met with lie chiefly along the southern coasts of Devonshire. Thus, in the cliffs near Torquay, the observer may see myriads of fossil corals in relief against the face of the rock. At Newton Abbot, in the limestone quarries, he may obtain trilobites, such as *Bronteus*, characteristic of this formation; and a rich assortment of other organisms. Again, at Plymouth, Chudleigh, Ashburton, Ipplepen, and wherever quarries are opened in the Devonian limestone, fossils may be obtained. At Pilton, Barnstaple, Ilfracombe, and Lynton, in North Devonshire, in the slate, sandstone, and limestone strata, there is plentiful supply of brachiopods, cephalopods, and trilobites.

The Old Red Sandstone may be regarded as the lacustrine equivalent of the marine strata distinguished as Devonian. In many places in Scotland, where quarries are opened in the sandstones, we may obtain remains of the remarkable fishes which lived during this epoch. Among other localities where these fossils are to be found, we may mention Carmoylie, in Forfarshire, Caithness (where the flagstones are frequently crowded with splendid and often entire specimens of *Osteolepis*), Cromarty, Moray, Nairn, and Gamrie in Banff. At Dura Den, near Coupar, in Fife, a very large number of huge fossil fishes have been found, and the specimens look remarkably well on the surfaces of the yellow sandstones.

At Kiltorcan, in Ireland, there is a wonderful abundance of the beautiful Devonian fern (*Palæopteris hibernicus*), and other vegetable fossils, as well as of the bivalve mollusca *Anodonta*. The remains of fishes are identical with those found in the Old Red Sandstone of Scotland.

The Carboniferous formation is of immense thickness, and as it has been much disturbed by faults, and been repeatedly jerked up to the surface, it occupies a very large superficial area in Great Britain. Hence there are numerous outcrops of all its subdivisions, and plenty of localities where the geological student may find the characteristic fossils, animal and vegetable, of each subdivision. Beginning with perhaps the richest and most interesting from a palæontological point of view—the carboniferous limestone,—we may mention the following localities as eminently rich in the fossils peculiar to this stratum :—Clifton, near Bristol, for fossil corals ; the Eglwyseg Rocks near Llangollen for brachiopods (*Producta*) and reef-building corals ; Hafod, about a mile and a half from Corwen, where we find a small "outlier" of the main mass of limestone forming the Eglwysegs. This quarry is perhaps the richest in Britain for number and variety of fossils. Among others the collector finds the beautiful *Phillipsastrea*. Fossil corals are to be found in every degree of development and age. Other capital collecting-grounds are the outcrops of the limestone strata near Castleton, in the Peak of Derbyshire, where are an abundance of encrinites, brachiopods, gasteropods, bivalves, cephalopods (especially *Goniatites sphæricus*), and such trilobites as *Phillipsia* ; but comparatively few reef-building corals. The best locality in Britain for the latter is perhaps the outcrop of the carboniferous limestone on the road from Mold to Denbigh, in North Wales. The very walls by the roadsides are nothing but geological museums. Near

Bakewell, in Derbyshire, we have an abundance of encrinites, although they are not even there so plentiful as a locality about a mile beyond Clitheroe, in Lancashire. This locality is an excellent collecting-ground, and at Salt Hill close by, in the shales dividing the limestone masses, there may be found any quantity of that small but pretty, and "last of the trilobites," *Phillipsia*.

The Yoredale shales are often crowded with fossils, nd as these shales part like a pile of cardboards, and the fossils are frequently converted into iron pyrites, they look as if they had been electrotyped on the black surfaces. These fossils consist of *Aviculo-Pecten, Goniatites, Nautilus, Posidonia,* &c. The best collecting localities are the outcrops of these shales along the banks of the streams which come down to Hebden Bridge, in Yorkshire, from the high ground towards Halifax. Here and there bands of black limestone occur in these shales, and they are full of minute and very beautiful fossil nuivalve and cephalopodous shells. Along the flanks of Pendle Hill, near Clitheroe, at Glossop, and abundantly at Lisdoonvarna, County Clare (where the "spas" derive their medicinal virtues from the water oozing through the Yoredale shales and dissolving the sulphites out of them), and in most places, indeed, where regular outcrops of these strata are seen fossils may be found. The lower coal-measures, near Oldham, in Lancashire, have beds of shale overlying the true but indifferent seam of coal, full of *marine* fossils. This is unusual, for the shale stratum forming the "roofs" of coal-seams are usually crowded with fossil ferns and when shells are present, they are generally representatives of fresh-water forms, as *Anthracosia*, &c. But this marine character of the *lower* seams of coal in Lancashire and Yorkshire is very general. Among the most notable of the fossils found there, often in great perfection and abundance, and usually in the condition of impure iron pyrites, is *Goniatites Listeri*.

We can hardly go to the many coal-pits, and examine the hillocks of shales pitched out, either in sinking the shafts deeper or in taking down the roofs, without finding an abundance of fossil ferns, club-mosses, molluscs, and fishes. In the neighbourhood of Manchester, as at Bolton, Clifton, Ashton, Woodley, Hyde, &c., fossil ferns are very abundant and beautifully preserved; as are also the *Calamites*, *Sigillaria*, *Lepidodendron*, &c., together with their catkins or *Lepidostrobus*. In a quarry on the road between Manchester and Bolton, at Peel Delph, the sandstone rock looks like a huge plum-pudding, it is so abundantly stocked with the fossil fruits of a coniferous tree allied to the *Salisburia* from Japan. These fruits are of a three-cornered shape, and have long been known by the name of *Trigonocarpum*.

Fossil bivalve mollusca (*Anthracosia*, &c.) are very numerous near Hyde and Wigan, where they form bands. At Carron, in Scotland, these shells have been converted into carbonate of iron, and the celebrated "Black band" ironstone is therefore nothing but a seam of these chemically-altered fossils. Near St. Helen's, in Lancashire, and in many parts of the North Staffordshire coal-field, but particularly near Longton, the shales abound in fossil fishes. In the little iron-stone nodules found among the shales on the refuse-heaps the student may possibly find an entire specimen, if he break the nodule open properly. In similar nodules found among the shales near the mines at Coalbrook-dale, in Shropshire, fossil king-crabs have been discovered. The neighbourhood of Newcastle is rich in fossil ferns; and at Jarrow colliery, in Ireland, some very remarkable remains of amphibians are occasionally exhumed.

The Permian rocks are richest in fossils near Tynemouth, where *Productus horridus* is to be found. At Collyhurst, Manchester, during excavations for the erection of house, &c., the Permian marls are laid open, and an abundance of *Schizodus*, &c., may there be picked up.

The New Red sandstone will yield the student very vivid impressions of foot-prints at Storeton quarry, near Birkenhead; at Lymm, in Cheshire; at Elgin and Lammermuir, in Scotland. In the neighbourhood of Leicester, in the upper Keuper beds, may be got *pseudomorphs* of rock-salt cubes, sun-cracks, impressions of rain-drops, &c.

The Rhætic strata are full of fossils, especially in the well-known section at Aust, on the Somersetshire side of the river Severn, nearly opposite Chepstow, where the beds may be seen resting on those of the New Red sandstone. Masses of the Rhætic rock lie at the base of the cliffs, and at low water the student may here hammer out an abundance of teeth of *Hybodus, Acrodus, Saurichthys*, &c., as well as such characteristic shells as *Pecten valoniensis, Ostrea Liassica*, &c. Lower down the estuary, on the other side, at Penarth, near Cardiff, the headland is composed of Rhætic strata, and there also may easily be disinterred a rich collection of fossil remains.

The Lias strata (as well as the Oolitic) run across England in a broad diagonal band, extending from the Yorkshire to the Dorsetshire coasts. The Lias often underlies flat ground, because its soft shales easily weather down. In such places no fossils will be found, except where deep excavations have been made. In the neighbourhood of Leicester, as at Barrow-on-Soar, Loughborough, &c., pits have been sunk in these strata to get at the bands of argillaceous limestone which are met with in the shales. There a rich harvest of remarkable fossils may be reaped, such as entire heads of *Ichthyosauri*, perfect specimens of ganoid fish, as *Dapedius*, &c., and *Ammonites* in abundance. In the escarpments of harder and generally limestone rocks which overlie these plains, a greater number and variety of Lias fossils may be more easily obtained; and where these strata form sea-cliffs, as at Whitby, in Yorkshire, and Lyme Regis, in Dorsetshire, enormous numbers of *Ammonites, Nautili, Belemnites, Pectens, Avicula*, &c., are easily exhumed.

The Oolite is a very various formation, and each of its rock varieties is more or less marked by peculiar fossils. This is noticeably so in the *lower* Oolite, where we have zones containing each peculiar Ammonites. Near Cheltenham, Middlesbrough, Scarborough, Northampton, Bath, and throughout

Lincolnshire, these beds extend, and they are very generally rich in fossils. As a great many excavations have been made in them, either to extract ironstone, limestone for burning into mortar, or buildingstones, it follows that there are more than usually numerous advantages offered to the young geologist in an "Oolitic" country to see sections and obtain fossils. Among the best places in England where Oolitic fossils can be obtained we mention the following: — Dundry Hill, near Bristol; Gristhorpe, near Scarborough (for fossil ferns, &c.); Stonesfield, at the slate-quarries; Collyweston, near Stamford; Cheltenham, and many parts of Gloucestershire, but particularly the neighbourhood of Stroud, Cirencester, Tetbury, and Minchinhampton; neighbourhood of Northampton (in ironstone); Chippenham, Hartwell, Tisbury, Portland, Isle of Purbeck, &c. At these various places the fossils of the different subdivisions of the Oolitic system may be obtained. At Burton Bradstock we shall find an abundance of superior Oolitic fossils. Stonesfield, in Oxfordshire, has long been famous for its fossil plants, corals, echinoderms, mollusca, fishes, reptilian, and even mammalian remains, and these are usually well preserved on the surfaces of the flaggy slates. The latter are quarried in the Evenlode valley, at Sarsden, Woodstock, Sevenhampton common, and Eyeford. On Minchinhampton common we may find an abundance of fossils of the Great Oolite, and also near the Seven Springs, North Leach, Burford, and Sherborne Park, in Gloucestershire. In the Portland beds we have the largest of fossil *Ammonites*, some of them being three feet in diameter. In the "dirt beds" (ancient soils) found intercalated amid the Purbeck beds we have fossil trunks and stools of coniferous and cycadeous trees, the latter of which are better known among the workmen by the name of "Crows' nests."

The Wealden strata require to be worked by somebody living on the spot for many fossils to be found. The wandering geologist may, however, meet with the remnants of fossil wood, and even reptilian remains, at the junction of the Hastings sand and Weald clay, as at Crickfield, where we have disinterred the teeth of *Iguanodon*. Near Battle we come across the lower beds of the Wealden series, so full of fossil shells as often to form flaggy limestones. The Tilgate stone has been celebrated for its yield of fossil reptilian remains ever since the days of Dr. Mantell; and Mr. H. B. Woodward tells us, that "it becomes a regular bone-bed in places." At various localities in Sussex, where the Weald clay occurs, there are beds of fresh-water shells, chiefly composed of *Paludinæ*, which are popularly known by the name of "Sussex Marble." These "marbles" are worked near Biddenden, Staplehurst, Crowhurst, Chiddingfold, Betworth, Bethersden, and Laughton; and the young geologist may obtain any number of these beautiful fossils at the above localities. At Horsham, Itchingfield, West Grinstead, &c., the beds of calcareous sandstones are not only ripple-marked, but impressed with the feet of *Iguanodon*. As the pedestrian walks from Hastings to Battle Abbey, along what was anciently a Roman road, he may easily perceive, from the ripple-marked flagstones of the causeway, that he is walking over the shallow portions of the delta where the Wealden strata were originally deposited.

The lower cretaceous beds are in places crowded with peculiar fossils, and, as a rule, they are in such an excellent state of preservation that few look better in the cabinet. As a rule, also, they are not difficult to extract. In the neighbourhood of Farringdon we find an area covered by the well-known "Sponge-gravel," in which is an abundance of such genera of fossil sponges as *Manon*, *Verticillipora*, *Scyphia*, &c. In Bedfordshire and Cambridgeshire the lower Green Sand is worked for " coprolite" stones; and there we find an abundance of phosphatized shells, teeth, bones, wood, &c., nearly all of them derivative, however, and chiefly from the Wealden and Oolitic strata. The Gault clay preserves the fossils beautifully, and the *Ammonites, Baculites, Hamites*, &c., are frequently quite iridescent when first laid open to the view. Not unfrequently the cephalopod shells are converted into iron pyrites.

Folkestone and the neighbourhood have long been noted for the abundance of these fossils. At Hunstanton, in Norfolk, there is a band of bright red chalk, overlaid by the white chalk, which causes the cliff to assume a very well-marked and easily-identified appearance out at sea. This red chalk is believed to be of the same age as the Gault. It contains many of the same kind of fossils; among others, numbers of the small *Belemnites minimus*. The Upper Green Sand in the Isle of Wight, and elsewhere, contains plenty of fossils. The most beautiful of all, however, are perhaps those obtained from the white chalk. They consist of fossil fishes, often most beautifully preserved, but requiring much time and patience to develop them, as the reader will see from Dr. Mantell's very full instructions as to how to proceed in this matter. The chalk of Sussex, Isle of Wight, and Kent, may be studied for signs and tokens of fossil fish wherever there is a quarry, and remains (chiefly teeth) of the large marine lizard *Mososaurus*. Everywhere there are to be obtained any number of bivalves (*Pecten, Spondylus, Inoceramus*, &c.) ; as well as brachiopods (*Terebratula carinata, T. obesa, Rhynchonella*, &c.), and *Belemnites*. Star-fishes, *Ananchytes, Micraster*, &c. In the white chalk near Norwich the latter are very abundant, and may always be obtained of the lime-burners at the pits, or dug out of the solid face of the chalk by the student himself.

The heaps of flint nodules excavated from the chalk and thrown aside in heaps, to be subsequently broken up, should always be carefully looked over by the student, for there are very often beautiful fossil shells and simple corals (as *Parasmilia*, &c.), imbedded in the flint, evidently when the latter was in a soft state. At Margate, Ramsgate, Dover, Croydon, Oxstead, Marden, Purley, Kenley, and elsewhere, may be obtained *Micraster, Holaster, Galerites, Ammonites*, &c.

The Tertiary strata are all well represented in Great Britain, with the exception of the Miocene. In the London Clay we have the island of Sheppy, in places a mass of fossil palm fruits (*Nipadites*), and many other fossils. In the plastic clay at Peckham is the *Paludina* bed, so called because full of that shell.

At the Charlton chalk-pits, close to the railway station, there may be obtained not only quantities of Cretaceous fossils, but also many from the Lower Eocene beds which may be seen capping the chalk.

The London clay is of course the chief and most important member of our English Eocene formation, being 500 feet in thickness. In certain places an extensive variety of fossils may be dug out; but Sheppy is undoubtedly the best locality. Near Harwich large *Nautili*, and the carapaces of huge turtles are frequently found. At Bognor, in Sussex, fossils can be collected, as well as in the Isle of Wight, in Alum and Whitecliffe bays. At Studland, Poole, Alum Bay, and Bournemouth (but especially at the latter place), there are "Leaf-beds," from which remains of many kinds of subtropical land plants have been extracted. At Bracklesham Bay, in Sussex, and also in the cliffs at Alum Bay, there are beds crowded with *Cardita* and *Turritella*. Barton and Hordwell, in Hampshire, yield most beautiful fossil marine shells, such as *Rostellaria*, *Voluta*, *Typhis*, *Crassatella*, &c. At Headon, Osborne, Bembridge, East Cowes, and elsewhere in the Isle of Wight, the student may easily obtain a most varied collection of fresh-water, brackish, and marine mollusca, of Upper Eocene age.

The Miocene beds of Bovey Tracey will hardly repay the student, and even if he should obtain any fossils thence, it is probable he would be disappointed at their being so badly preserved. In Suffolk, however, underlying the Coralline as well as the Red Crags, are roundish or oval masses of sandstone, locally known as "Box-stones," used for mending the roads with. These are broken up and rounded fragments of an Upper Miocene or very early Pliocene stratum, which still extends unbroken beneath many parts of Belgium. The geologist finds many fossils in these Box-stones, and they are most abundant about Felixstowe and Foxhall, near Ipswich, in Suffolk.

The "Crag" beds are famous collecting-grounds—none better. To geologize in a crag-pit is like examining the bed of the sea after the water has been drained off. The young student soon fills his boxes with sharks' teeth, corals, univalve and bivalve shells, &c., wherever the crag crops out. The fossils can be extracted almost with the finger and thumb, and thirty or forty species be obtained at almost any pit in little over an hour. The Crags are three in number—the Coralline, Red, and Norwich. The best places for obtaining the fossil polyzoa (formerly called *Corallines*) from the first-mentioned deposit are at Aldborough, Sudbourne (especially at the pits near Sir Richard Wallace's Park), and around Oxford generally. The Red Crag has a much larger extension; and as phosphatic nodules, called "coprolites," are worked from it at its base, a good many sections are opened between Ipswich and Felixstowe. Many men are employed at these pits, from whom teeth of deer, rhinoceros, tapir, fragments of *Mastodon*, &c., may be purchased. The shells are particularly abundant, especially *Pectunculus*, *Astarte*, and the famous left-handed red whelk, *Fusus contrarius.* The best localities for getting Red Crag fossils are at Bentley, Foxhall, and Bucklesham, near Ipswich; and at Butley, Waldringfield, Kirton, Falkenham, Nacton, and Felixstowe. At the latter place the crag forms steep cliffs, full of shells, fifty feet high.

The Norwich Crag has two beds, an upper and a lower, the former being remarkable for the large number of Arctic mollusca it contains. This upper bed is best seen, and the largest number of fossils can be got out of it, at Chillesford, near Orford, in Suffolk. At Aldeby the shells are most beautifully preserved, the bivalves being usually both together, and the mollusca occupying the same position in the sand-bed as when they were alive. At Bramerton, Postwich, and Thorpe, near Norwich, the bed of crag bearing the latter name is finely developed, and abundance of Pliocene shells can be obtained. At Wroxham, Sherringham, and elsewhere in Norfolk, a shell-bed of later date occurs, in which we find large numbers of the still living *Tellina Balthica.*

The Boulder-Clay beds rarely contain fossils of their own, but the student can always find abundant interest in them, by collecting the different kinds of rocks brought as boulders, noticing whence they have come from, their parent sources, what is their mineralogical composition, whether they are scratched and striated by glacial action, &c. Researches of this kind in the boulder clays are much wanted, and it is good work, in which every young collector might be profitably engaged.

CHAPTER XVII.

CONCLUSION.

At the close of the Glacial epoch Great Britain was not a group of islands, but a part of the European continent. It was at this stage that the animals and plants which are now indigenous took possession of the area and spread themselves over it, so that when the separation from the continent took place which split our country up into islands, the same fauna and flora had been distributed as was common to Europe generally. The only difference was that not quite so large a number of species had been spread. Our fresh-water fish, worms, mollusca, etc., are the same as those of continental rivers, and it is evident these could not have crossed the salt sea, but must have spread before England and Ireland became islands. It was probably about the end of what we may call the "continental era" of Great Britain that MAN first made his appearance. There is every geological reason for believing that he was in possession before the "island era" of our country began. That the splitting-up of Great Britain into islands is of a geologically recent occurrence we have every fact to assist us in believing. All round our coasts there are *submerged forests,* many of them far out at sea where the water is shallow. We may still see their ancient soils. The trees in many places are now extending their aged roots where they once grew. It is evident that if we were to elevate the sea-bed so as to raise these ancient forests high enough above the level of the sea to enable them to grow, we should not only make the seas which girdle our shores shallower, but actually convert their beds into dry land, and thus once more establish continental conditions; for there are few places in the German Ocean deep enough to cover the ball on the top of St. Paul's Cathedral, were that edifice placed in the sea! The same is true of the Irish Sea.

It would seem as if man first made his appearance in our country in the *savage* state. His flint implements are found imbedded in the river gravels off the then larger streams in whose waters he probably fished. The earliest of these implements are very rudely chipped (*palæolithic*), but we can see they are weapons; and they gradually pass into the more elegantly-cut and chipped and polished weapons of a later date (*neolithic*) by almost imperceptible degrees. Caves and holes of the earth then sheltered man from the pitiless blast. The hyæna, cave bear, woolly-haired mammoth, and hairy rhinoceros were his congeners; and it is possible that some of them owe their local, and perhaps entire, extinction to the vigour with which they were hunted down by the new-comer. The snows gathered thick and deep in winter months, although the glaciers no longer slid down the valleys, and the natural streams swelled when they melted, and carried down quantities of mud, sand, and stones. In this manner the *alluvium* of our rivers was spread out in sheets and layers wherever the ground was flatter than usual. River gravels banked up the sides of the streams in terraces, and as the weather gradually became milder, and the volume of water carried down by the streams smaller, the rivers shrank within narrower limits, and so left their old banks (terraces) high and dry.

Now took place that gradual depression of the lowlying, marshy plain, long characterized by boggy morass and stagnant tarns, which lay between the Norfolk and Suffolk coasts and Belgium. A tributary of the Thames had probably flowed northerly across this monotonous swamp, in that deep submarine valley which is marked on the Admiralty charts as the "Deep Water Channel." All this plain, as it sank, was encroached upon by the waters of the North Sea, whose abysmal depths show us plainly the length of time it has existed as an ocean. In this manner the sea gradually gained on the flat marshes until at length England was separated from the Continent. It is very probable that a similar geographical change had detached Ireland from England just before, and the reader will find the reasons for arriving at this conclusion in the study of the relative distribution of animals and plants towards the west.

Well, and rightly, have geologists distinguished the epoch when MAN makes his appearance as the *Quaternary*. All those physical changes we denominate *pre-historic* have occurred since he took possession of the globe. Written history only goes authoritatively backward a few thousands of years, and even then we find a few comparatively civilised nations existing. All the rest, Britons among them, were sunk in the very depths of savagery and barbarism. A few thousand years *backward* still, and how low must have been the condition of humanity. A few thousand years *onward*, since written history commenced, and what a marvellous progress!

One cannot study this geological life-scheme of our globe, badly put together though it is on account of the necessary imperfection of the record, without seeing a unity of plan throughout. The last geological epoch which preceded the appearance of man, put the finishing touches to the surface of our old planet. The stones had been formed that should build man's house, the coals had been stored away that should warm his hearth, the metals had been segregated into veins, or gathered into pockets; the animals and plants of the world had been broken up and distributed over zones and into regions never occupied before. And now the subsoils of the temperate regions, where civilization should hereafter be best and most highly developed, where Christianity could be established and join civilisation hand in hand in issuing forth to the uttermost parts of the earth—had been prepared by the formation of clays and sands unknown before, so that such highly-favoured regions are now best able to support the nations whose leisure can be devoted to loftier and nobler engagements! The words of the inspired writer fitly express the conclusions arrived at by the reverent geologist: "God Himself formed the earth and made it; He hath established it; He created it not in vain, He formed it to be inhabited."

THE END.

Society for Promoting Christian Knowledge.

NATURAL HISTORY RAMBLES.

Fcap. 8vo., Illustrated, Cloth boards, 2s. 6d. each.

LAKES AND RIVERS.
By C. O. GROOM NAPIER, F.G.S., Author of "The Food, Use, and Beauty of British Birds," &c., &c.

LANE AND FIELD.
By the Rev. J. G. WOOD, M.A., Author of "Homes without Hands," &c., &c.

MOUNTAIN AND MOOR.
By J. E. TAYLOR, F.L.S., F.G.S., Editor of "Science-Gossip."

THE SEA-SHORE.
By Professor P. MARTIN DUNCAN, M.B. (London), F.R.S., Honorary Fellow of King's College, London.

THE WOODLANDS.
By M. C. COOKE, M.A., LL.D.

UNDERGROUND.
By J. E. TAYLOR, F.L.S., F.G.S., Editor of "Science-Gossip."

	s.	d.

Beauty in Common Things. Illustrated by 12 Drawings from Nature, by Mrs. J. W. Whymper, and printed in Colours, with descriptions by the Author of "Life Underground," &c. 4to. ....*Cloth boards* 10 6

Botanical Rambles. By the late Rev. C. A. JOHNS, B.A., F.L.S. With illustrations and woodcuts. Royal 16mo...*Cloth boards* 2 0

British Animals. With 12 coloured plates. 16mo. *Ornamental covers* 1 6

Birds of the Sea-shore. With 12 coloured plates. 18mo ....*Cloth boards* 1 8

Forest Trees (The) of Great Britain. By the Rev. C. A. JOHNS, B.A., F.L.S. New Edition. With 150 woodcuts. Post 8vo. .... *Cloth boards* 5 0

Natural History of the Bible (The). By the Rev. CANON TRISTRAM, Author of "The Land of Israel," &c. With numerous illustrations. Crown 8vo. *Cloth boards* 7 6

Animal Creation (The). A popular Introduction to Zoology. By THOMAS RYMER JONES, F.R.S. With 488 woodcuts. Post 8vo. .... *Cloth boards* 7 6

Lessons from the Animal World. By CHARLES and SARAH TOMLINSON. With 162 woodcuts, in two volumes. Fcap. 8vo. .... *Cloth boards* 4 0

Birds' Nests and Eggs. With 22 coloured plates of Eggs. Square 16mo. .... *Cloth boards* 3 0

British Birds in their Haunts. By the late Rev. C. A. JOHNS, B.A., F.L.S. With 190 engravings by Wolf and Whymper. Post 8vo. .... *Cloth boards* 10 0

	s.	d.
Flowers of the Field. By the late Rev. C. A. JOHNS, B.A., F.L.S. With numerous woodcuts. Fcap. 8vo. .... *Cloth boards*	5	0
Wild Flowers. By ANNE PRATT, Author of "Our Native Songsters," &c. With 192 coloured plates, in two volumes. 16mo. .... *Cloth boards*	16	0
Evenings at the Microscope; or, Researches among the Minuter Organs and Forms of Animal Life. By P. H. GOSSE, F.R.S. A new Edition revised and annotated. With 112 woodcuts. Post 8vo. ...*Cloth boards*	4	0
Familiar History of British Fishes. By FRANK BUCKLAND, Inspector of Salmon Fisheries for England and Wales. With a Frontispiece and 134 woodcuts. Crown 8vo. .... *Cloth boards*	5	0
Natural History (Illustrated Sketches of): consisting of Descriptions and Engravings of Animals. With numerous woodcuts, in 2 vols. Fcap. 8vo. Series I. and II. .... *Cloth boards, each Vol.*	2	6
Our Native Songsters. By ANNE PRATT, Author of "Wild Flowers." With 72 coloured plates. 16mo. *Cloth boards*	8	0
Selborne (The Natural History of). By the Rev. GILBERT WHITE. With Frontispiece, Map, and 50 woodcuts. Post 8vo. .... *Cloth boards*	2	6
Ocean (The). By PHILIP HENRY GOSSE, F.R.S., Author of "Evenings at the Microscope." With 51 illustrations and woodcuts. Post 8vo. *Cloth boards*	4	6
Dew-drop and the Mist (The): an Account of the Phenomena and Properties of Atmospheric Vapour in various Parts of the World. By C. TOMLINSON, F.C.S. With woodcuts and diagrams. Fcap. 8vo. ...*Cloth boards*	2	6

	s.	d.

Frozen Stream (*The*): an Account of the Formation and Properties of Ice in various Parts of the World. By CHARLES TOMLINSON. With woodcuts and diagrams. Fcap. 8vo. ....*Cloth boards* 1 6

Rain-Cloud and Snow-Storm: an Account of the Nature, Formation, Properties, Dangers, and Uses of Rain and Snow. By C. TOMLINSON. With numerous woodcuts and diagrams. Fcap. 8vo. *Cloth boards* 2 6

Tempest (*The*): an Account of the Origin and Phenomena of Wind in various Parts of the World. By CHARLES TOMLINSON. With numerous woodcuts and diagrams. Fcap. 8vo. ....*Cloth boards* 2 6

Thunder-Storm (*The*): an Account of the Properties of Lightning and of Atmospheric Electricity in various Parts of the World. By CHARLES TOMLINSON. With numerous woodcuts and diagrams. Fcap. 8vo. *Cloth boards* 2 6

Winter in the Arctic Regions and Summer in the Antarctic Regions. By CHARLES TOMLINSON. With two maps, and several illustrations and woodcuts. Crown 8vo. ....*Cloth boards* 4 0

Depositories:

77, GREAT QUEEN STREET, LINCOLN'S-INN FIELDS, W.C.;
4, ROYAL EXCHANGE, E.C.; AND 48, PICCADILLY, W.,
LONDON.

www.ingramcontent.com/pod-product-compliance
Lightning Source LLC
Chambersburg PA
CBHW021346230426
43666CB00006B/430